Decoding the TOEFL® iBT

Actual Test

WRITING 2

INTRODUCTION

For many learners of English, the TOEFL® iBT will be the most important standardized test they ever take. Unfortunately for a large number of these individuals, the material covered on the TOEFL® iBT remains a mystery to them, so they are unable to do well on the test. We hope that by using the *Decoding the TOEFL® iBT* series, individuals who take the TOEFL® iBT will be able to excel on the test and, in the process of using the book, may unravel the mysteries of the test and therefore make the material covered on the TOEFL® iBT more familiar to themselves.

The TOEFL® iBT covers the four main skills that a person must learn when studying any foreign language: reading, listening, speaking, and writing. The *Decoding the TOEFL® iBT* series contains books that cover all four of these skills. The *Decoding the TOEFL® iBT* series contains books with three separate levels for all four of the topics, and it also contains *Decoding the TOEFL® iBT Actual Test* books. These books contain several actual tests that learners can utilize to help them become better prepared to take the TOEFL® iBT. This book, *Decoding the TOEFL® iBT Actual Test Writing 2*, covers the writing aspect of the test and includes both integrated and independent tasks that are arranged in the same format as the TOEFL® iBT. Finally, the TOEFL® iBT underwent a number of changes in August 2019. This book—and the others in the series—takes those changes into account and incorporates them in the texts and questions, so readers of this second edition can be assured that they have up-to-date knowledge of the test.

Decoding the TOEFL® iBT Actual Test Writing 2 can be used by learners who are taking classes and also by individuals who are studying by themselves. It contains a total of fifteen full-length writing actual tests. Each actual test contains an integrated task (writing an essay based on reading and listening) and an independent task (writing an essay based on knowledge and experience). All of the passages and lectures that are used in the tasks are the same length and have the same difficulty levels as those found on the TOEFL® iBT. In addition, the tasks contain the same types of questions that appear on the actual TOEFL® iBT. Individuals who use *Decoding the TOEFL® iBT Actual Test Writing 2* will therefore be able to prepare themselves not only to take the TOEFL® iBT but also to perform well on the test.

We hope that everyone who uses *Decoding the TOEFL® iBT Actual Test Writing 2* will be able to become more familiar with the TOEFL® iBT and will additionally improve his or her score on the test. As the title of the book implies, we hope that learners can use it to crack the code on the TOEFL® iBT, to make the test itself less mysterious and confusing, and to get the highest score possible. Finally, we hope that both learners and instructors can use this book to its full potential. We wish all of you the best of luck as you study English and prepare for the TOEFL® iBT, and we hope that *Decoding the TOEFL® iBT Actual Test Writing 2* can provide you with assistance during the course of your studies.

Michael A. Putlack
Stephen Poirier

TABLE
OF
CONTENTS

ABOUT THE TOEFL® iBT WRITING SECTION

How the Section Is Organized

The writing section is the last part of the TOEFL® iBT and consists of two portions: the Integrated Writing Task and the Independent Writing Task. The Integrated Writing Task requires test takers to explain how a short reading passage and lecture are related while the Independent Writing Task requires test takers to explain their opinions about a given situation. Test takers have 20 minutes to complete the Integrated Writing Task. For the Independent Writing Task, they have 30 minutes.

The writing section tests the ability of test takers to organize information clearly. The responses do not have to be creative or original. They just need to be succinct and direct. The most important thing test takers can do to boost their score is to present their ideas clearly by using relevant examples. Strong support and vivid details are essential for earning a top score.

Changes in the Writing Section

There are no major changes in the Writing section. However, in the Independent Writing Task, the directions tend to be longer than before on average. The question also often asks not only about a general opinion but also about a specific situation. This can be seen as a measure to prevent test takers from writing memorized essays. At the end of the question, there are directions that prohibit the writing of a memorized example. Therefore, it is important that test takers practice writing essays based on their own ideas instead of trying to memorize model essays.

Question Types

TYPE 1 The Integrated Writing Task

The Integrated Writing Task consists of three parts. Test takers begin by reading a passage approximately 230 to 300 words in length for 3 minutes. Following this, test takers listen to a lecture that either supports or contradicts the reading. Finally, test takers are given 20 minutes to write their essays. The essays should be between 150 and 225 words in length. During this time, the reading passage will reappear on the computer screen. Again, it is important to remember that test takers are not expected to present any new ideas in their essays. Instead, test takers must summarize the lecture and explain its relationship with the reading passage by providing examples from both.

ABOUT THE
TOEFL® iBT
WRITING SECTION

There are five possible writing tasks test takers will be presented with, but they all require test takers to summarize the lecture and to explain how it either supports or contradicts the reading.

If the listening passage challenges or contradicts the reading passage, the tasks will be presented in one of the following ways:

- Summarize the points made in the lecture, being sure to explain how they cast doubt on specific points made in the reading passage.
  cf. This question type accounts for most of the questions that have been asked on the TOEFL® iBT so far.
- Summarize the points made in the lecture, being sure to explain how they challenge specific claims/arguments made in the reading passage.
- Summarize the points made in the lecture, being sure to specifically explain how they answer the problems raised in the reading passage.

If the listening passage supports or strengthens the reading passage, the tasks will be presented in one of the following ways:

- Summarize the points made in the lecture, being sure to specifically explain how they support the explanations in the reading passage.
- Summarize the points made in the lecture, being sure to specifically explain how they strengthen specific points made in the reading passage.

TYPE 2 The Independent Writing Task

The Independent Writing Task is the second half of the TOEFL® iBT writing section. Test takers have 30 minutes to write an essay explaining their options about a given question. Typically, an effective response is between 300 and 400 words in length. In order to earn a top score, test takers must clearly present their ideas by using logical arguments and effective supporting examples. Strong responses generally include an introductory paragraph with a clear thesis statement, two or three supporting paragraphs with focused topic sentences, and a brief concluding paragraph.

There are three possible writing tasks you will be presented with, but they all ask you to express your opinion about an important issue.

For the agree/disagree type, the task will be presented in the following way:

- Do you agree or disagree with the following statement?
  [A sentence or sentences that present an issue]
  Use specific reasons and examples to support your answer.
  cf. This question type accounts for most of the essay topics that have been asked on the TOEFL® iBT so far.

For the preference type, the task will be presented in the following way:

- Some people prefer X. Others prefer Y. Which do you prefer? Use specific reasons and examples to support your choice.

For the opinion type, the task will be presented in the following way:

- [A sentence or sentences that state a fact]
  In your opinion, what is one thing that should be . . . ? Use specific reasons and examples to support your answer.

Actual Test

01

Writing Section Directions

 Make sure your headset is on.

This section measures your ability to use writing to communicate in an academic environment. There will be two writing tasks.

For the first writing task, you will read a passage and listen to a lecture and then answer a question based on what you have read and heard. For the second writing task, you will answer a question based on your own knowledge and experience.

Now listen to the directions for the first writing task.

Writing Based on Reading and Listening

For this task, you will first have **3 minutes** to read a passage about an academic topic. You may take notes on the passage if you wish. The passage will then be removed and you will listen to a lecture about the same topic. While you listen, you may also take notes.

Then you will have **20 minutes** to write a response to a question that asks you about the relationship between the lecture you heard and the reading passage. Try to answer the question as completely as possible using information from the reading passage and the lecture. The question does **not** ask you to express your personal opinion. You will be able to see the reading passage again when it is time for you to write. You may use your notes to help you answer the question.

Typically, an effective response will be 150 to 225 words long. Your response will be judged on the quality of your writing and on the completeness and accuracy of the content. If you finish your response before time is up, you may click on **NEXT** to go on to the second writing task.

Now you will see the reading passage for 3 minutes. Remember it will be available to you again when you are writing. Immediately after the reading time ends, the lecture will begin, so keep your headset on until the lecture is over.

Due to the country's size, the fastest way to travel between most cities in the United States is by airplane. However, many rural regions of the country are rather far from the large airports that serve major commercial airlines. Prior to the deregulation of the airline industry in 1978, the federal government required major airlines to provide service to smaller, more remote airports even if those routes were unprofitable. After deregulation occurred, the airlines planned to shut down many of those routes until the government stepped in and began subsidizing them with the Essential Air Service (EAS).

The EAS benefits the people residing in rural areas in a number of ways. First, it pays airlines to fly small 19-seat commuter aircraft from airports in areas with small populations to bigger airports two to four times each day. At present, the EAS operates at more than 160 rural airports around the country. These airports are all at least 110 kilometers away from a major airport and are much farther away from larger metropolises in many cases.

Thanks to the EAS, passengers in remote areas can pay affordable prices for the tickets they purchase. The government subsidizes each seat on these planes, which enables airlines to charge lower rates to their passengers. The original subsidy paid up to $200 per ticket, but that has increased in recent years to allow for inflation.

Finally, regular airline service to secluded communities helps improve the economies of many of these places. For instance, it provides employment for the people who work at the airport and offer services at those places. Many of these airports also have businesses that give flying lessons to individuals and connect small communities with one another, which benefits these places economically.

AT01-01

Directions You have 20 minutes to plan and write your response. Your response will be judged on the basis of the quality of your writing and on how well your response presents the points in the lecture and their relationship to the passage. Typically, an effective response will be 150-225 words.

Question Summarize the points made in the lecture, being sure to explain how they challenge specific claims made in the reading passage.

COPY   CUT   PASTE   Word Count : 0

Due to the country's size, the fastest way to travel between most cities in the United States is by airplane. However, many rural regions of the country are rather far from the large airports that serve major commercial airlines. Prior to the deregulation of the airline industry in 1978, the federal government required major airlines to provide service to smaller, more remote airports even if those routes were unprofitable. After deregulation occurred, the airlines planned to shut down many of those routes until the government stepped in and began subsidizing them with the Essential Air Service (EAS).

The EAS benefits the people residing in rural areas in a number of ways. First, it pays airlines to fly small 19-seat commuter aircraft from airports in areas with small populations to bigger airports two to four times each day. At present, the EAS operates at more than 160 rural airports around the country. These airports are all at least 110 kilometers away from a major airport and are much farther away from larger metropolises in many cases.

Thanks to the EAS, passengers in remote areas can pay affordable prices for the tickets they purchase. The government subsidizes each seat on these planes, which enables airlines to charge lower rates to their passengers. The original subsidy paid up to $200 per ticket, but that has increased in recent years to allow for inflation.

Finally, regular airline service to secluded communities helps improve the economies of many of these places. For instance, it provides employment for the people who work at the airport and offer services at those places. Many of these airports also have businesses that give flying lessons to individuals and connect small communities with one another, which benefits these places economically.

VOLUME

HELP

NEXT

HIDE TIME 00:20 :00

COPY   CUT   PASTE

Word Count : 0

Writing Based on Knowledge and Experience

For this task, you will write an essay in response to a question that asks you to state, explain, and support your opinion on an issue. You have **30 minutes** to write your essay.

Typically, an effective essay will contain a minimum of 300 words. Your essay will be judged on the quality of your writing. This includes the development of your ideas, the organization of the content, and the quality and accuracy of the language you used to express ideas.

Click on **CONTINUE** to go on.

COPY   CUT   PASTE   Word Count : 0

Directions Read the question below. You have 30 minutes to plan, write, and revise your essay. Typically, an effective response will contain a minimum of 300 words.

Question

These days, more and more people are getting pets such as dogs and cats. They also frequently spend large amounts of money on their pets instead of making purchases on items that they need for themselves.

Do you agree or disagree that people spend too much money on their pets when they should be using the money in other ways? Use specific reasons and examples to support your answer.

Be sure to use your own words. Do not use memorized examples.

VOLUME

HELP

NEXT

HIDE TIME 00:30:00

COPY CUT PASTE

Word Count : 0

Actual Test

02

Writing Section Directions

 Make sure your headset is on.

This section measures your ability to use writing to communicate in an academic environment. There will be two writing tasks.

For the first writing task, you will read a passage and listen to a lecture and then answer a question based on what you have read and heard. For the second writing task, you will answer a question based on your own knowledge and experience.

Now listen to the directions for the first writing task.

Writing Based on Reading and Listening

For this task, you will first have **3 minutes** to read a passage about an academic topic. You may take notes on the passage if you wish. The passage will then be removed and you will listen to a lecture about the same topic. While you listen, you may also take notes.

Then you will have **20 minutes** to write a response to a question that asks you about the relationship between the lecture you heard and the reading passage. Try to answer the question as completely as possible using information from the reading passage and the lecture. The question does **not** ask you to express your personal opinion. You will be able to see the reading passage again when it is time for you to write. You may use your notes to help you answer the question.

Typically, an effective response will be 150 to 225 words long. Your response will be judged on the quality of your writing and on the completeness and accuracy of the content. If you finish your response before time is up, you may click on **NEXT** to go on to the second writing task.

Now you will see the reading passage for 3 minutes. Remember it will be available to you again when you are writing. Immediately after the reading time ends, the lecture will begin, so keep your headset on until the lecture is over.

There are many types of nyctinastic plants, which are plants whose leaves close up when night falls and reopen in the morning. Some nyctinastic plants are members of the pea, wood sorrel, arrowroot, and caltrop families while individual examples include the mimosa, acacia, ginger, and shamrock plants. The leaves typically fold into a vertical position with pairs of leaves facing one another while being close together. Botanists are unsure why these plants behave in this manner, but they have several theories regarding it.

One theory accepted by numerous botanists is that the closing of leaves allows water to flow to critical areas of the plants. Once the leaves fold up, any water droplets on them can trickle down to the plants' stems and roots, where water is needed. In addition, the downward flow of water prevents too much moisture from accumulating on the leaves. This may help inhibit the growth of harmful fungi on the leaves, which could damage or kill the plant.

In the 1800s, Charles Darwin came up with his own theory regarding this behavior. He believed that plants folded their leaves at night to avoid freezing temperatures. When the leaves were folded, the surface area of each individual leaf that was exposed to the elements was reduced greatly, which therefore kept cold weather from causing harm to the leaves.

A third hypothesis is that the folding of leaves aids predators. When the leaves of plants close at night, this allows predators to see more easily. As a result, they can identify prey and kill it more easily. Many of the prey that these predators kill eat the leaves of plants, so this action by plants assists predators, which, in turn, help plants by ridding them of some animals that consume their leaves.

Directions You have 20 minutes to plan and write your response. Your response will be judged on the basis of the quality of your writing and on how well your response presents the points in the lecture and their relationship to the passage. Typically, an effective response will be 150-225 words.

Question Summarize the points made in the lecture, being sure to explain how they cast doubt on specific points made in the reading passage.

COPY   CUT   PASTE   Word Count : 0

There are many types of nyctinastic plants, which are plants whose leaves close up when night falls and reopen in the morning. Some nyctinastic plants are members of the pea, wood sorrel, arrowroot, and caltrop families while individual examples include the mimosa, acacia, ginger, and shamrock plants. The leaves typically fold into a vertical position with pairs of leaves facing one another while being close together. Botanists are unsure why these plants behave in this manner, but they have several theories regarding it.

One theory accepted by numerous botanists is that the closing of leaves allows water to flow to critical areas of the plants. Once the leaves fold up, any water droplets on them can trickle down to the plants' stems and roots, where water is needed. In addition, the downward flow of water prevents too much moisture from accumulating on the leaves. This may help inhibit the growth of harmful fungi on the leaves, which could damage or kill the plant.

In the 1800s, Charles Darwin came up with his own theory regarding this behavior. He believed that plants folded their leaves at night to avoid freezing temperatures. When the leaves were folded, the surface area of each individual leaf that was exposed to the elements was reduced greatly, which therefore kept cold weather from causing harm to the leaves.

A third hypothesis is that the folding of leaves aids predators. When the leaves of plants close at night, this allows predators to see more easily. As a result, they can identify prey and kill it more easily. Many of the prey that these predators kill eat the leaves of plants, so this action by plants assists predators, which, in turn, help plants by ridding them of some animals that consume their leaves.

Writing Based on Knowledge and Experience

For this task, you will write an essay in response to a question that asks you to state, explain, and support your opinion on an issue. You have **30 minutes** to write your essay.

Typically, an effective essay will contain a minimum of 300 words. Your essay will be judged on the quality of your writing. This includes the development of your ideas, the organization of the content, and the quality and accuracy of the language you used to express ideas.

Click on **CONTINUE** to go on.

COPY CUT PASTE

Word Count : 0

Directions Read the question below. You have 30 minutes to plan, write, and revise your essay. Typically, an effective response will contain a minimum of 300 words.

Question

Some people believe that going on regular field trips is an ideal way to educate students. Others prefer that students stay at school and receive all of their learning in classrooms.

Which method would you prefer? Use specific reasons and examples to support your answer.

Be sure to use your own words. Do not use memorized examples.

COPY CUT PASTE Word Count : 0

Actual Test

03

Writing Section Directions

 Make sure your headset is on.

This section measures your ability to use writing to communicate in an academic environment. There will be two writing tasks.

For the first writing task, you will read a passage and listen to a lecture and then answer a question based on what you have read and heard. For the second writing task, you will answer a question based on your own knowledge and experience.

Now listen to the directions for the first writing task.

Writing Based on Reading and Listening

For this task, you will first have **3 minutes** to read a passage about an academic topic. You may take notes on the passage if you wish. The passage will then be removed and you will listen to a lecture about the same topic. While you listen, you may also take notes.

Then you will have **20 minutes** to write a response to a question that asks you about the relationship between the lecture you heard and the reading passage. Try to answer the question as completely as possible using information from the reading passage and the lecture. The question does **not** ask you to express your personal opinion. You will be able to see the reading passage again when it is time for you to write. You may use your notes to help you answer the question.

Typically, an effective response will be 150 to 225 words long. Your response will be judged on the quality of your writing and on the completeness and accuracy of the content. If you finish your response before time is up, you may click on **NEXT** to go on to the second writing task.

Now you will see the reading passage for 3 minutes. Remember it will be available to you again when you are writing. Immediately after the reading time ends, the lecture will begin, so keep your headset on until the lecture is over.

Many American corn farmers have problems with rootworms, pests which attack their crops. Rootworms start as eggs in the ground and subsequently hatch as larvae in spring. These larvae eat the small roots of corn plants and, after becoming bigger, burrow into the larger roots before turning into adult beetles. The adults crawl out of the ground and feed on the leaves of the corn plants before the females lay their eggs in July. It is estimated that up to eighteen percent of all corn crops are destroyed due to rootworms each year. These losses—combined with the costs of efforts to control rootworms—cause American farmers to lose approximately one billion dollars annually.

Fortunately, farmers presently utilize three effective ways of dealing with rootworms. The best method is crop rotation. Essentially, farmers grow corn in their fields one year but leave those fields fallow the next. This deprives rootworm larvae of food, so they die soon after hatching. Since no rootworms will grow to become adults, the next year, corn can be planted in the fields without any fear of a rootworm infestation.

Planting corn earlier in spring is another effective method. This gives the corn more time to grow, so the plants' roots are bigger when the rootworms hatch. The roots' larger sizes make them less edible to the larvae. An additional benefit is that the corn pollinates before the rootworms become adults. Adult rootworm beetles prefer laying their eggs in non-pollinated fields, so fewer eggs get laid.

Insecticides are yet another method to control rootworm populations. Both powder and liquid insecticides are effective against eggs and larvae if they are directly applied at the base of each plant. The mass spraying of insecticides, which is the method most farmers prefer, can eradicate adult rootworm beetles, too.

AT03-01

Directions You have 20 minutes to plan and write your response. Your response will be judged on the basis of the quality of your writing and on how well your response presents the points in the lecture and their relationship to the passage. Typically, an effective response will be 150-225 words.

Question Summarize the points made in the lecture, being sure to explain how they cast doubt on specific points made in the reading passage.

COPY   CUT   PASTE   Word Count : 0

Many American corn farmers have problems with rootworms, pests which attack their crops. Rootworms start as eggs in the ground and subsequently hatch as larvae in spring. These larvae eat the small roots of corn plants and, after becoming bigger, burrow into the larger roots before turning into adult beetles. The adults crawl out of the ground and feed on the leaves of the corn plants before the females lay their eggs in July. It is estimated that up to eighteen percent of all corn crops are destroyed due to rootworms each year. These losses—combined with the costs of efforts to control rootworms—cause American farmers to lose approximately one billion dollars annually.

Fortunately, farmers presently utilize three effective ways of dealing with rootworms. The best method is crop rotation. Essentially, farmers grow corn in their fields one year but leave those fields fallow the next. This deprives rootworm larvae of food, so they die soon after hatching. Since no rootworms will grow to become adults, the next year, corn can be planted in the fields without any fear of a rootworm infestation.

Planting corn earlier in spring is another effective method. This gives the corn more time to grow, so the plants' roots are bigger when the rootworms hatch. The roots' larger sizes make them less edible to the larvae. An additional benefit is that the corn pollinates before the rootworms become adults. Adult rootworm beetles prefer laying their eggs in non-pollinated fields, so fewer eggs get laid.

Insecticides are yet another method to control rootworm populations. Both powder and liquid insecticides are effective against eggs and larvae if they are directly applied at the base of each plant. The mass spraying of insecticides, which is the method most farmers prefer, can eradicate adult rootworm beetles, too.

Writing Based on Knowledge and Experience

For this task, you will write an essay in response to a question that asks you to state, explain, and support your opinion on an issue. You have **30 minutes** to write your essay.

Typically, an effective essay will contain a minimum of 300 words. Your essay will be judged on the quality of your writing. This includes the development of your ideas, the organization of the content, and the quality and accuracy of the language you used to express ideas.

Click on **CONTINUE** to go on.

COPY CUT PASTE Word Count : 0

Directions Read the question below. You have 30 minutes to plan, write, and revise your essay. Typically, an effective response will contain a minimum of 300 words.

Question

Students often have homework assignments in multiple classes at the same time. They must therefore determine how they will spend their time completing all of their assignments.

Do you agree or disagree that it is better to complete one homework assignment and then start another than to work on several homework assignments at the same time? Use specific reasons and examples to support your answer.

Be sure to use your own words. Do not use memorized examples.

VOLUME   HELP   NEXT

HIDE TIME 00:30:00

COPY   CUT   PASTE

Word Count : 0

Actual Test

04

Writing Section Directions

 Make sure your headset is on.

This section measures your ability to use writing to communicate in an academic environment. There will be two writing tasks.

For the first writing task, you will read a passage and listen to a lecture and then answer a question based on what you have read and heard. For the second writing task, you will answer a question based on your own knowledge and experience.

Now listen to the directions for the first writing task.

Writing Based on Reading and Listening

For this task, you will first have **3 minutes** to read a passage about an academic topic. You may take notes on the passage if you wish. The passage will then be removed and you will listen to a lecture about the same topic. While you listen, you may also take notes.

Then you will have **20 minutes** to write a response to a question that asks you about the relationship between the lecture you heard and the reading passage. Try to answer the question as completely as possible using information from the reading passage and the lecture. The question does **not** ask you to express your personal opinion. You will be able to see the reading passage again when it is time for you to write. You may use your notes to help you answer the question.

Typically, an effective response will be 150 to 225 words long. Your response will be judged on the quality of your writing and on the completeness and accuracy of the content. If you finish your response before time is up, you may click on **NEXT** to go on to the second writing task.

Now you will see the reading passage for 3 minutes. Remember it will be available to you again when you are writing. Immediately after the reading time ends, the lecture will begin, so keep your headset on until the lecture is over.

The Bible describes many actual historical places, one of which is the city of Ophir, which was reputed to be fabulously wealthy. According to the Old Testament, King Solomon sent a fleet of ships from a port on the Red Sea to Ophir. The fleet later returned with a large shipment of gold, silver, gems, ivory, sandalwood, peacocks, and apes. Modern-day scholars, however, are uncertain where Ophir was located as it no longer exists. Two leading candidates for its location are Africa and India.

Supporters of Africa being the location of Ophir state that there are two possible sites on the continent's east coast. The first is in modern-day Zimbabwe while the second is in Ethiopia. In the past, Zimbabwe was noted for being a center of gold production in sub-Saharan Africa. Today, some believe that a large area there with ruins may have been the location of Ophir. Meanwhile, there are others who think that the ancestors of the Afar people of Ethiopia founded Ophir. They cite the similarities between the names Ophir and Afar for their belief.

The case for India is based partially upon the length of the voyage of King Solomon's fleet. The Old Testament notes that it took three years for the fleet to complete the trip. This implies a longer trip than one to the east coast of Africa. Many have suggested that the fleet sailed deep into the Indian Ocean. Several places in India have names that sound similar to Ophir as do some groups of ancient people. In addition, many places in southern India were noted for their gold, ivory, peacocks, and apes. Finally, the only known major source of sandalwood during that period was southern India, which makes it the leading candidate for the location of Ophir.

AT04-01

Directions You have 20 minutes to plan and write your response. Your response will be judged on the basis of the quality of your writing and on how well your response presents the points in the lecture and their relationship to the passage. Typically, an effective response will be 150-225 words.

Question Summarize the points made in the lecture, being sure to explain how they challenge specific arguments made in the reading passage.

COPY   CUT   PASTE   Word Count : 0

The Bible describes many actual historical places, one of which is the city of Ophir, which was reputed to be fabulously wealthy. According to the Old Testament, King Solomon sent a fleet of ships from a port on the Red Sea to Ophir. The fleet later returned with a large shipment of gold, silver, gems, ivory, sandalwood, peacocks, and apes. Modern-day scholars, however, are uncertain where Ophir was located as it no longer exists. Two leading candidates for its location are Africa and India.

Supporters of Africa being the location of Ophir state that there are two possible sites on the continent's east coast. The first is in modern-day Zimbabwe while the second is in Ethiopia. In the past, Zimbabwe was noted for being a center of gold production in sub-Saharan Africa. Today, some believe that a large area there with ruins may have been the location of Ophir. Meanwhile, there are others who think that the ancestors of the Afar people of Ethiopia founded Ophir. They cite the similarities between the names Ophir and Afar for their belief.

The case for India is based partially upon the length of the voyage of King Solomon's fleet. The Old Testament notes that it took three years for the fleet to complete the trip. This implies a longer trip than one to the east coast of Africa. Many have suggested that the fleet sailed deep into the Indian Ocean. Several places in India have names that sound similar to Ophir as do some groups of ancient people. In addition, many places in southern India were noted for their gold, ivory, peacocks, and apes. Finally, the only known major source of sandalwood during that period was southern India, which makes it the leading candidate for the location of Ophir.

Writing Based on Knowledge and Experience

For this task, you will write an essay in response to a question that asks you to state, explain, and support your opinion on an issue. You have **30 minutes** to write your essay.

Typically, an effective essay will contain a minimum of 300 words. Your essay will be judged on the quality of your writing. This includes the development of your ideas, the organization of the content, and the quality and accuracy of the language you used to express ideas.

Click on **CONTINUE** to go on.

COPY   CUT   PASTE   Word Count : 0

Directions Read the question below. You have 30 minutes to plan, write, and revise your essay. Typically, an effective response will contain a minimum of 300 words.

Question

A university recently decided to offer classes on foreign cultures to its students. It is also planning to make these classes required for all of its students to take before they can graduate.

Do you agree or disagree that it should be mandatory for universities to teach students about other cultures? Use specific reasons and examples to support your answer.

Be sure to use your own words. Do not use memorized examples.

COPY CUT PASTE

Word Count : 0

Actual Test

05

Writing Section Directions

 Make sure your headset is on.

This section measures your ability to use writing to communicate in an academic environment. There will be two writing tasks.

For the first writing task, you will read a passage and listen to a lecture and then answer a question based on what you have read and heard. For the second writing task, you will answer a question based on your own knowledge and experience.

Now listen to the directions for the first writing task.

Writing Based on Reading and Listening

For this task, you will first have **3 minutes** to read a passage about an academic topic. You may take notes on the passage if you wish. The passage will then be removed and you will listen to a lecture about the same topic. While you listen, you may also take notes.

Then you will have **20 minutes** to write a response to a question that asks you about the relationship between the lecture you heard and the reading passage. Try to answer the question as completely as possible using information from the reading passage and the lecture. The question does **not** ask you to express your personal opinion. You will be able to see the reading passage again when it is time for you to write. You may use your notes to help you answer the question.

Typically, an effective response will be 150 to 225 words long. Your response will be judged on the quality of your writing and on the completeness and accuracy of the content. If you finish your response before time is up, you may click on **NEXT** to go on to the second writing task.

Now you will see the reading passage for 3 minutes. Remember it will be available to you again when you are writing. Immediately after the reading time ends, the lecture will begin, so keep your headset on until the lecture is over.

Automatic traffic camera systems are frequently placed in positions alongside highways and on city streets where they can observe traffic. Their cameras have built-in radar systems that can detect if vehicles are exceeding the speed limit, and some can determine if vehicles run red lights at intersections. Whenever one of these cameras takes a picture of a traffic violator, the vehicle's owner is sent a picture of the violation and is fined a certain amount of money. Even though many people dislike traffic cameras, they provide numerous advantages in the municipalities that employ them.

The primary advantage of traffic cameras is that they require people to obey traffic laws in order to avoid being ticketed. This, in turn, has reduced the number of traffic accidents in various places. Statistics in a large number of American cities have proven that many high-risk intersections have seen a reduction in traffic accidents since traffic cameras were introduced.

A second advantage is that the cameras generate a large amount of income for both the cities and states using them. The money comes from the fines violators have to pay. In most cases, the income is spent on worthwhile projects to enhance local communities. For instance, some cities and states spend the fine money on libraries while others use it for public education.

Yet another benefit of traffic cameras is that they can accurately record traffic violations which occur. The cameras photograph the offending vehicles' license plates and record the speeds they were going or when they ran red lights. Many cameras take pictures of the drivers as well. These pictures provide solid proof that the drivers broke the law, so the courts can feel confident they are not making mistakes when issuing fines to lawbreakers.

Directions You have 20 minutes to plan and write your response. Your response will be judged on the basis of the quality of your writing and on how well your response presents the points in the lecture and their relationship to the passage. Typically, an effective response will be 150-225 words.

Question Summarize the points made in the lecture, being sure to explain how they challenge specific arguments made in the reading passage.

| COPY | CUT | PASTE | Word Count : 0 |

Automatic traffic camera systems are frequently placed in positions alongside highways and on city streets where they can observe traffic. Their cameras have built-in radar systems that can detect if vehicles are exceeding the speed limit, and some can determine if vehicles run red lights at intersections. Whenever one of these cameras takes a picture of a traffic violator, the vehicle's owner is sent a picture of the violation and is fined a certain amount of money. Even though many people dislike traffic cameras, they provide numerous advantages in the municipalities that employ them.

The primary advantage of traffic cameras is that they require people to obey traffic laws in order to avoid being ticketed. This, in turn, has reduced the number of traffic accidents in various places. Statistics in a large number of American cities have proven that many high-risk intersections have seen a reduction in traffic accidents since traffic cameras were introduced.

A second advantage is that the cameras generate a large amount of income for both the cities and states using them. The money comes from the fines violators have to pay. In most cases, the income is spent on worthwhile projects to enhance local communities. For instance, some cities and states spend the fine money on libraries while others use it for public education.

Yet another benefit of traffic cameras is that they can accurately record traffic violations which occur. The cameras photograph the offending vehicles' license plates and record the speeds they were going or when they ran red lights. Many cameras take pictures of the drivers as well. These pictures provide solid proof that the drivers broke the law, so the courts can feel confident they are not making mistakes when issuing fines to lawbreakers.

COPY CUT PASTE

Word Count : 0

Writing Based on Knowledge and Experience

For this task, you will write an essay in response to a question that asks you to state, explain, and support your opinion on an issue. You have **30 minutes** to write your essay.

Typically, an effective essay will contain a minimum of 300 words. Your essay will be judged on the quality of your writing. This includes the development of your ideas, the organization of the content, and the quality and accuracy of the language you used to express ideas.

Click on **CONTINUE** to go on.

COPY CUT PASTE

Word Count : 0

Directions Read the question below. You have 30 minutes to plan, write, and revise your essay. Typically, an effective response will contain a minimum of 300 words.

Question

If you could change one thing to improve your health, which of the following would you alter: the quality of the food you eat, the amount of exercise you get, or the amount of stress in your life? Use specific reasons and examples to support your answer.

Be sure to use your own words. Do not use memorized examples.

COPY   CUT   PASTE

Actual Test

06

Writing Section Directions

 Make sure your headset is on.

This section measures your ability to use writing to communicate in an academic environment. There will be two writing tasks.

For the first writing task, you will read a passage and listen to a lecture and then answer a question based on what you have read and heard. For the second writing task, you will answer a question based on your own knowledge and experience.

Now listen to the directions for the first writing task.

Writing Based on Reading and Listening

For this task, you will first have **3 minutes** to read a passage about an academic topic. You may take notes on the passage if you wish. The passage will then be removed and you will listen to a lecture about the same topic. While you listen, you may also take notes.

Then you will have **20 minutes** to write a response to a question that asks you about the relationship between the lecture you heard and the reading passage. Try to answer the question as completely as possible using information from the reading passage and the lecture. The question does **not** ask you to express your personal opinion. You will be able to see the reading passage again when it is time for you to write. You may use your notes to help you answer the question.

Typically, an effective response will be 150 to 225 words long. Your response will be judged on the quality of your writing and on the completeness and accuracy of the content. If you finish your response before time is up, you may click on **NEXT** to go on to the second writing task.

Now you will see the reading passage for 3 minutes. Remember it will be available to you again when you are writing. Immediately after the reading time ends, the lecture will begin, so keep your headset on until the lecture is over.

Since the 1980s, more than 200 species of frogs have disappeared from the planet and become extinct. This is unfortunate since frogs are essential to their ecosystems for a variety of reasons. For instance, they help control the insect population, especially disease-carrying insects such as mosquitoes, they are a vital part of the food chain for numerous reptiles, birds, fish, and mammals, and tadpoles—baby frogs—help keep water clean by consuming algae. For the most part, humans are responsible for what is happening to frogs.

Global warming, which many experts believe is being exacerbated by humans, is a major problem for some species of frogs. Warmer temperatures are causing the extensive loss of the marshland habitats of countless frogs as these ecosystems disappear at an alarming rate. Frogs require water to lay their eggs in and for tadpoles to reside in until they reach adulthood. Yet hot weather is causing the ecosystems frogs live in to dry up and disappear.

Chemical pesticides and weed killers used by farmers also assume some blame. These chemicals seep into groundwater, which then flows into lowland marshes. The skin of frogs is porous, so it easily absorbs these chemicals, which kill the frogs. Banning the usage of these chemicals is essential to frogs' survival.

Another issue is that sick frogs are being transported worldwide. Frogs are collected in some countries and then sold as pets, food, and medical research animals in other nations. Individual frogs are rarely tested for infectious diseases, such as chytridiomycosis, which is caused by a type of fungus, though. This disease has spread so far and wide that scientists blame it for the extinction of up to 100 species of frogs. Unless regulations are enacted to prevent future outbreaks of diseases, the global frog population will surely continue to plummet.

AT06-01

Directions You have 20 minutes to plan and write your response. Your response will be judged on the basis of the quality of your writing and on how well your response presents the points in the lecture and their relationship to the passage. Typically, an effective response will be 150-225 words.

Question Summarize the points made in the lecture, being sure to explain how they challenge specific claims made in the reading passage.

COPY   CUT   PASTE   Word Count : 0

Since the 1980s, more than 200 species of frogs have disappeared from the planet and become extinct. This is unfortunate since frogs are essential to their ecosystems for a variety of reasons. For instance, they help control the insect population, especially disease-carrying insects such as mosquitoes, they are a vital part of the food chain for numerous reptiles, birds, fish, and mammals, and tadpoles—baby frogs—help keep water clean by consuming algae. For the most part, humans are responsible for what is happening to frogs.

Global warming, which many experts believe is being exacerbated by humans, is a major problem for some species of frogs. Warmer temperatures are causing the extensive loss of the marshland habitats of countless frogs as these ecosystems disappear at an alarming rate. Frogs require water to lay their eggs in and for tadpoles to reside in until they reach adulthood. Yet hot weather is causing the ecosystems frogs live in to dry up and disappear.

Chemical pesticides and weed killers used by farmers also assume some blame. These chemicals seep into groundwater, which then flows into lowland marshes. The skin of frogs is porous, so it easily absorbs these chemicals, which kill the frogs. Banning the usage of these chemicals is essential to frogs' survival.

Another issue is that sick frogs are being transported worldwide. Frogs are collected in some countries and then sold as pets, food, and medical research animals in other nations. Individual frogs are rarely tested for infectious diseases, such as chytridiomycosis, which is caused by a type of fungus, though. This disease has spread so far and wide that scientists blame it for the extinction of up to 100 species of frogs. Unless regulations are enacted to prevent future outbreaks of diseases, the global frog population will surely continue to plummet.

Writing Based on Knowledge and Experience

For this task, you will write an essay in response to a question that asks you to state, explain, and support your opinion on an issue. You have **30 minutes** to write your essay.

Typically, an effective essay will contain a minimum of 300 words. Your essay will be judged on the quality of your writing. This includes the development of your ideas, the organization of the content, and the quality and accuracy of the language you used to express ideas.

Click on **CONTINUE** to go on.

COPY   CUT   PASTE

Word Count : 0

Directions Read the question below. You have 30 minutes to plan, write, and revise your essay. Typically, an effective response will contain a minimum of 300 words.

Question

Do you agree or disagree with the following statement?

It is very important for family members to eat together regularly.

Use specific reasons and examples to support your answer.

Be sure to use your own words. Do not use memorized examples.

Actual Test

07

Writing Section Directions

 Make sure your headset is on.

This section measures your ability to use writing to communicate in an academic environment. There will be two writing tasks.

For the first writing task, you will read a passage and listen to a lecture and then answer a question based on what you have read and heard. For the second writing task, you will answer a question based on your own knowledge and experience.

Now listen to the directions for the first writing task.

Writing Based on Reading and Listening

For this task, you will first have **3 minutes** to read a passage about an academic topic. You may take notes on the passage if you wish. The passage will then be removed and you will listen to a lecture about the same topic. While you listen, you may also take notes.

Then you will have **20 minutes** to write a response to a question that asks you about the relationship between the lecture you heard and the reading passage. Try to answer the question as completely as possible using information from the reading passage and the lecture. The question does **not** ask you to express your personal opinion. You will be able to see the reading passage again when it is time for you to write. You may use your notes to help you answer the question.

Typically, an effective response will be 150 to 225 words long. Your response will be judged on the quality of your writing and on the completeness and accuracy of the content. If you finish your response before time is up, you may click on **NEXT** to go on to the second writing task.

Now you will see the reading passage for 3 minutes. Remember it will be available to you again when you are writing. Immediately after the reading time ends, the lecture will begin, so keep your headset on until the lecture is over.

Amtrak is the government-owned train passenger service in the United States. Operating since 1971, it provides rail service to most major American cities. Yet Amtrak is not the best way to travel since it does not service every state and city. Nor is Amtrak profitable as it costs American taxpayers millions—or even billions—of dollars every year. While Amtrak was expected to become profitable soon after being established, it has failed to turn an annual profit even once. The government should therefore privatize Amtrak, which would result in the elimination of the majority of Amtrak's problems.

The main problem for Amtrak is that, like the vast majority of government-run operations, there is a lack of quality service, which discourages passengers. The service on Amtrak has an incredibly poor reputation. Common complaints revolve around rude employees, slow trains, interrupted service with passengers having to continue their journeys by bus, and delayed and canceled trains. If Amtrak were to become a private company, its employees would no longer have secure government jobs but could instead by fired for negligence. This would encourage them to provide better service and to make sure that most of the problems associated with Amtrak no longer happen lest certain individuals lose their jobs.

Safety is another major issues since most of the railways, bridges, and tunnels used by Amtrak are outdated and in dire need of repair. Unfortunately, billions of dollars the government has given to Amtrak have gone toward upgrading the trains and raising salaries while more vital infrastructure is being ignored. This could lead to fatal accidents in the future. A private company would invest more money into improving the railroad's infrastructure. This would let it provide better and safer service, which would, in turn, attract more passengers and enabled the railroad to become profitable.

AT07-01

Directions You have 20 minutes to plan and write your response. Your response will be judged on the basis of the quality of your writing and on how well your response presents the points in the lecture and their relationship to the passage. Typically, an effective response will be 150-225 words.

Question Summarize the points made in the lecture, being sure to explain how they cast doubt on specific points made in the reading passage.

Amtrak is the government-owned train passenger service in the United States. Operating since 1971, it provides rail service to most major American cities. Yet Amtrak is not the best way to travel since it does not service every state and city. Nor is Amtrak profitable as it costs American taxpayers millions—or even billions—of dollars every year. While Amtrak was expected to become profitable soon after being established, it has failed to turn an annual profit even once. The government should therefore privatize Amtrak, which would result in the elimination of the majority of Amtrak's problems.

The main problem for Amtrak is that, like the vast majority of government-run operations, there is a lack of quality service, which discourages passengers. The service on Amtrak has an incredibly poor reputation. Common complaints revolve around rude employees, slow trains, interrupted service with passengers having to continue their journeys by bus, and delayed and canceled trains. If Amtrak were to become a private company, its employees would no longer have secure government jobs but could instead by fired for negligence. This would encourage them to provide better service and to make sure that most of the problems associated with Amtrak no longer happen lest certain individuals lose their jobs.

Safety is another major issues since most of the railways, bridges, and tunnels used by Amtrak are outdated and in dire need of repair. Unfortunately, billions of dollars the government has given to Amtrak have gone toward upgrading the trains and raising salaries while more vital infrastructure is being ignored. This could lead to fatal accidents in the future. A private company would invest more money into improving the railroad's infrastructure. This would let it provide better and safer service, which would, in turn, attract more passengers and enabled the railroad to become profitable.

Writing Based on Knowledge and Experience

For this task, you will write an essay in response to a question that asks you to state, explain, and support your opinion on an issue. You have **30 minutes** to write your essay.

Typically, an effective essay will contain a minimum of 300 words. Your essay will be judged on the quality of your writing. This includes the development of your ideas, the organization of the content, and the quality and accuracy of the language you used to express ideas.

Click on **CONTINUE** to go on.

COPY   CUT   PASTE   Word Count : 0

Directions Read the question below. You have 30 minutes to plan, write, and revise your essay. Typically, an effective response will contain a minimum of 300 words.

Question

Some people believe that it is better for colleagues or classmates to communicate in person when working on a project. Others prefer to do their communicating through email or over the telephone.

Which method do you prefer? Use specific reasons and examples to support your answer.

Be sure to use your own words. Do not use memorized examples.

Actual Test

08

Writing Section Directions

 Make sure your headset is on.

This section measures your ability to use writing to communicate in an academic environment. There will be two writing tasks.

For the first writing task, you will read a passage and listen to a lecture and then answer a question based on what you have read and heard. For the second writing task, you will answer a question based on your own knowledge and experience.

Now listen to the directions for the first writing task.

Writing Based on Reading and Listening

For this task, you will first have **3 minutes** to read a passage about an academic topic. You may take notes on the passage if you wish. The passage will then be removed and you will listen to a lecture about the same topic. While you listen, you may also take notes.

Then you will have **20 minutes** to write a response to a question that asks you about the relationship between the lecture you heard and the reading passage. Try to answer the question as completely as possible using information from the reading passage and the lecture. The question does **not** ask you to express your personal opinion. You will be able to see the reading passage again when it is time for you to write. You may use your notes to help you answer the question.

Typically, an effective response will be 150 to 225 words long. Your response will be judged on the quality of your writing and on the completeness and accuracy of the content. If you finish your response before time is up, you may click on **NEXT** to go on to the second writing task.

Now you will see the reading passage for 3 minutes. Remember it will be available to you again when you are writing. Immediately after the reading time ends, the lecture will begin, so keep your headset on until the lecture is over.

Around the world, it is possible to find certain rough-shaped ground formations that are called mima mounds. They are typically a few meters in diameter and one meter in height although the biggest ones can be up to fifty meters in diameter. They appear in small groups as well as in large numbers over a broad area. Mima mounds commonly form in flat, arid regions such as the Mima Prairie in the state of Washington in the United States. While experts have researched mima mounds for many years, how they are formed is a mystery that has long eluded them.

One possible explanation concerns the activity of plants. Plants in areas with mima mounds grow in one spot while their roots spread out into the surrounding soil beneath the surface. These plants then drain the surrounding land of water and nutrients, which keeps other plants from growing. Over time, these islands of plants capture soil blown in the air and prevent the erosion of the soil they are in. This results in the building of small plant islands that assume the appearances of mima mounds.

Seismic activity is a second popular suggested cause of mima mounds. Studies of earthquakes show that loose soil often re-forms in rounded piles during tremors. It is therefore possible that mima mounds are created when upheavals during earthquakes shake the ground in such a way that the soil gets arranged into piles.

There are also some individuals who subscribe to the theory that animals, particularly gophers, are responsible for making mima mounds. Gophers are animals that create extensive underground dens by pushing the soil up. Over a long period of time, it is speculated, their actions may result in the creating of mima mounds.

Directions You have 20 minutes to plan and write your response. Your response will be judged on the basis of the quality of your writing and on how well your response presents the points in the lecture and their relationship to the passage. Typically, an effective response will be 150-225 words.

Question Summarize the points made in the lecture, being sure to explain how they cast doubt on specific points made in the reading passage.

COPY   CUT   PASTE   Word Count : 0

Around the world, it is possible to find certain rough-shaped ground formations that are called mima mounds. They are typically a few meters in diameter and one meter in height although the biggest ones can be up to fifty meters in diameter. They appear in small groups as well as in large numbers over a broad area. Mima mounds commonly form in flat, arid regions such as the Mima Prairie in the state of Washington in the United States. While experts have researched mima mounds for many years, how they are formed is a mystery that has long eluded them.

One possible explanation concerns the activity of plants. Plants in areas with mima mounds grow in one spot while their roots spread out into the surrounding soil beneath the surface. These plants then drain the surrounding land of water and nutrients, which keeps other plants from growing. Over time, these islands of plants capture soil blown in the air and prevent the erosion of the soil they are in. This results in the building of small plant islands that assume the appearances of mima mounds.

Seismic activity is a second popular suggested cause of mima mounds. Studies of earthquakes show that loose soil often re-forms in rounded piles during tremors. It is therefore possible that mima mounds are created when upheavals during earthquakes shake the ground in such a way that the soil gets arranged into piles.

There are also some individuals who subscribe to the theory that animals, particularly gophers, are responsible for making mima mounds. Gophers are animals that create extensive underground dens by pushing the soil up. Over a long period of time, it is speculated, their actions may result in the creating of mima mounds.

Writing Based on Knowledge and Experience

For this task, you will write an essay in response to a question that asks you to state, explain, and support your opinion on an issue. You have **30 minutes** to write your essay.

Typically, an effective essay will contain a minimum of 300 words. Your essay will be judged on the quality of your writing. This includes the development of your ideas, the organization of the content, and the quality and accuracy of the language you used to express ideas.

Click on **CONTINUE** to go on.

COPY | CUT | PASTE | Word Count : 0

Directions Read the question below. You have 30 minutes to plan, write, and revise your essay. Typically, an effective response will contain a minimum of 300 words.

Question

Do you agree or disagree with the following statement?

The way a person dresses is a good indication of that individual's personality and character.

Use specific reasons and examples to support your answer.

Be sure to use your own words. Do not use memorized examples.

Actual Test

09

Writing Section Directions

 Make sure your headset is on.

This section measures your ability to use writing to communicate in an academic environment. There will be two writing tasks.

For the first writing task, you will read a passage and listen to a lecture and then answer a question based on what you have read and heard. For the second writing task, you will answer a question based on your own knowledge and experience.

Now listen to the directions for the first writing task.

Writing Based on Reading and Listening

For this task, you will first have **3 minutes** to read a passage about an academic topic. You may take notes on the passage if you wish. The passage will then be removed and you will listen to a lecture about the same topic. While you listen, you may also take notes.

Then you will have **20 minutes** to write a response to a question that asks you about the relationship between the lecture you heard and the reading passage. Try to answer the question as completely as possible using information from the reading passage and the lecture. The question does **not** ask you to express your personal opinion. You will be able to see the reading passage again when it is time for you to write. You may use your notes to help you answer the question.

Typically, an effective response will be 150 to 225 words long. Your response will be judged on the quality of your writing and on the completeness and accuracy of the content. If you finish your response before time is up, you may click on **NEXT** to go on to the second writing task.

Now you will see the reading passage for 3 minutes. Remember it will be available to you again when you are writing. Immediately after the reading time ends, the lecture will begin, so keep your headset on until the lecture is over.

In the 1930s, vast areas of the Great Plains region in the United States suffered one of history's worst-recorded droughts. Known as the Dust Bowl due to the dust storms associated with it, the disaster caused severe hardship for untold numbers of individuals. While the lack of rainfall over a several-year period caused the drought, it was exacerbated by the farmers who were most negatively affected by it.

In the 1920s, the aftermath of the Russian Revolution caused Russia no longer to be a global supplier of foodstuffs. This led to an increased demand for American wheat abroad. American farmers therefore began breaking more ground to plant as much wheat as possible. In that decade, as many as five million acres of land on the Great Plains started being used for agriculture. Unfortunately, the soil conditions in most of those places were unsuitable for farming, a fact well known at the time. The topsoil was dry and sandy and required sufficient moisture to stay clumped together. When less rain fell in the 1930s, the soil became worthless for farming, and much of the land became barren.

In the 1890s, there had been another serious drought in the region, and that time was still within living memory of most farmers in the 1930s. Yet they failed to take measures necessary to protect the topsoil from erosion. For instance, farmers could have planted trees to act as wind breaks to cut down on wind erosion. They could have also let some land remain fallow each season, which would have enabled prairie grasses to regrow and thus anchor the soil to the ground. They failed, however, to act responsibly, so much of the once-valuable topsoil was blown away by the wind, which resulted in dust storms and made the land worthless for farming.

AT09-01

Directions You have 20 minutes to plan and write your response. Your response will be judged on the basis of the quality of your writing and on how well your response presents the points in the lecture and their relationship to the passage. Typically, an effective response will be 150-225 words.

Question Summarize the points made in the lecture, being sure to explain how they challenge specific arguments made in the reading passage.

COPY   CUT   PASTE   Word Count : 0

In the 1930s, vast areas of the Great Plains region in the United States suffered one of history's worst-recorded droughts. Known as the Dust Bowl due to the dust storms associated with it, the disaster caused severe hardship for untold numbers of individuals. While the lack of rainfall over a several-year period caused the drought, it was exacerbated by the farmers who were most negatively affected by it.

In the 1920s, the aftermath of the Russian Revolution caused Russia no longer to be a global supplier of foodstuffs. This led to an increased demand for American wheat abroad. American farmers therefore began breaking more ground to plant as much wheat as possible. In that decade, as many as five million acres of land on the Great Plains started being used for agriculture. Unfortunately, the soil conditions in most of those places were unsuitable for farming, a fact well known at the time. The topsoil was dry and sandy and required sufficient moisture to stay clumped together. When less rain fell in the 1930s, the soil became worthless for farming, and much of the land became barren.

In the 1890s, there had been another serious drought in the region, and that time was still within living memory of most farmers in the 1930s. Yet they failed to take measures necessary to protect the topsoil from erosion. For instance, farmers could have planted trees to act as wind breaks to cut down on wind erosion. They could have also let some land remain fallow each season, which would have enabled prairie grasses to regrow and thus anchor the soil to the ground. They failed, however, to act responsibly, so much of the once-valuable topsoil was blown away by the wind, which resulted in dust storms and made the land worthless for farming.

COPY CUT PASTE

Word Count : 0

Writing Based on Knowledge and Experience

For this task, you will write an essay in response to a question that asks you to state, explain, and support your opinion on an issue. You have **30 minutes** to write your essay.

Typically, an effective essay will contain a minimum of 300 words. Your essay will be judged on the quality of your writing. This includes the development of your ideas, the organization of the content, and the quality and accuracy of the language you used to express ideas.

Click on **CONTINUE** to go on.

VOLUME HELP NEXT

HIDE TIME 00:30:00

COPY CUT PASTE

Word Count : 0

Directions Read the question below. You have 30 minutes to plan, write, and revise your essay. Typically, an effective response will contain a minimum of 300 words.

Question

Do you agree or disagree with the following statement?

Getting advice from friends who are older than you is better than getting advice from friends who are the same age as you.

Use specific reasons and examples to support your answer.

Be sure to use your own words. Do not use memorized examples.

COPY   CUT   PASTE

Word Count : 0

Actual Test

10

Writing Section Directions

 Make sure your headset is on.

This section measures your ability to use writing to communicate in an academic environment. There will be two writing tasks.

For the first writing task, you will read a passage and listen to a lecture and then answer a question based on what you have read and heard. For the second writing task, you will answer a question based on your own knowledge and experience.

Now listen to the directions for the first writing task.

Writing Based on Reading and Listening

For this task, you will first have **3 minutes** to read a passage about an academic topic. You may take notes on the passage if you wish. The passage will then be removed and you will listen to a lecture about the same topic. While you listen, you may also take notes.

Then you will have **20 minutes** to write a response to a question that asks you about the relationship between the lecture you heard and the reading passage. Try to answer the question as completely as possible using information from the reading passage and the lecture. The question does **not** ask you to express your personal opinion. You will be able to see the reading passage again when it is time for you to write. You may use your notes to help you answer the question.

Typically, an effective response will be 150 to 225 words long. Your response will be judged on the quality of your writing and on the completeness and accuracy of the content. If you finish your response before time is up, you may click on **NEXT** to go on to the second writing task.

Now you will see the reading passage for 3 minutes. Remember it will be available to you again when you are writing. Immediately after the reading time ends, the lecture will begin, so keep your headset on until the lecture is over.

For a brief period millions of years ago, dinosaurs and primitive mammals lived side by side. The fossil evidence indicates that most early mammals were herbivores; however, some evidence shows that at least one species was a carnivore that fed upon small dinosaurs. This animal, a small catlike mammal, was *Repenomamus robustus*, or *R. robustus* for short. Many paleontologists were unsure if it was a scavenger or hunter until a fossil of *R. robustus* was found in China in 2005. This fossil included the remains of a baby dinosaur called the psittacosaur in its body, suggesting that the animal had been eaten.

A close examination of both specimens reveals that *R. robustus* was not a hunter but was instead a scavenger of dinosaurs. The primary reason concerned its size. *R. robustus* was smaller than most dinosaur species alive during its day, so it was highly unlikely to attack them. While the fossilized *R. robustus* had consumed a psittacosaur, that animal was a baby so was much smaller than an adult psittacosaur.

The body shape of *R. robustus* also proves it was not a hunter. It had short legs and a squat body, neither feature of which provided it with any speed. Its legs were more on the outside of its body rather than beneath it, so it must have run with an awkward gait. Thus it would have been unable successfully to chase down and kill any dinosaurs.

Finally, there were no teeth marks on the bones of the baby psittacosaur. This fact indicates that the baby dinosaur was not attacked and then killed and chewed on. While *R. robustus* had sharp teeth and strong jaws, the absence of teeth marks on the bones suggests it did not kill the psittacosaur but instead came across the animal after it had died.

🎧 AT10-01

Directions You have 20 minutes to plan and write your response. Your response will be judged on the basis of the quality of your writing and on how well your response presents the points in the lecture and their relationship to the passage. Typically, an effective response will be 150-225 words.

Question Summarize the points made in the lecture, being sure to explain how they cast doubt on specific points made in the reading passage.

COPY   CUT   PASTE   Word Count : 0

For a brief period millions of years ago, dinosaurs and primitive mammals lived side by side. The fossil evidence indicates that most early mammals were herbivores; however, some evidence shows that at least one species was a carnivore that fed upon small dinosaurs. This animal, a small catlike mammal, was *Repenomamus robustus*, or *R. robustus* for short. Many paleontologists were unsure if it was a scavenger or hunter until a fossil of *R. robustus* was found in China in 2005. This fossil included the remains of a baby dinosaur called the psittacosaur in its body, suggesting that the animal had been eaten.

A close examination of both specimens reveals that *R. robustus* was not a hunter but was instead a scavenger of dinosaurs. The primary reason concerned its size. *R. robustus* was smaller than most dinosaur species alive during its day, so it was highly unlikely to attack them. While the fossilized *R. robustus* had consumed a psittacosaur, that animal was a baby so was much smaller than an adult psittacosaur.

The body shape of *R. robustus* also proves it was not a hunter. It had short legs and a squat body, neither feature of which provided it with any speed. Its legs were more on the outside of its body rather than beneath it, so it must have run with an awkward gait. Thus it would have been unable successfully to chase down and kill any dinosaurs.

Finally, there were no teeth marks on the bones of the baby psittacosaur. This fact indicates that the baby dinosaur was not attacked and then killed and chewed on. While *R. robustus* had sharp teeth and strong jaws, the absence of teeth marks on the bones suggests it did not kill the psittacosaur but instead came across the animal after it had died.

Writing Based on Knowledge and Experience

For this task, you will write an essay in response to a question that asks you to state, explain, and support your opinion on an issue. You have **30 minutes** to write your essay.

Typically, an effective essay will contain a minimum of 300 words. Your essay will be judged on the quality of your writing. This includes the development of your ideas, the organization of the content, and the quality and accuracy of the language you used to express ideas.

Click on **CONTINUE** to go on.

VOLUME   HELP   NEXT

HIDE TIME 00:30:00

COPY   CUT   PASTE   Word Count : 0

Directions Read the question below. You have 30 minutes to plan, write, and revise your essay. Typically, an effective response will contain a minimum of 300 words.

Question

Do you agree or disagree with the following statement?

Children ages five to ten should be required to study art and music in addition to math, language, science, and history.

Use specific reasons and examples to support your answer.

Be sure to use your own words. Do not use memorized examples.

COPY CUT PASTE

Word Count : 0

Actual Test

11

Writing Section Directions

 Make sure your headset is on.

This section measures your ability to use writing to communicate in an academic environment. There will be two writing tasks.

For the first writing task, you will read a passage and listen to a lecture and then answer a question based on what you have read and heard. For the second writing task, you will answer a question based on your own knowledge and experience.

Now listen to the directions for the first writing task.

Writing Based on Reading and Listening

For this task, you will first have **3 minutes** to read a passage about an academic topic. You may take notes on the passage if you wish. The passage will then be removed and you will listen to a lecture about the same topic. While you listen, you may also take notes.

Then you will have **20 minutes** to write a response to a question that asks you about the relationship between the lecture you heard and the reading passage. Try to answer the question as completely as possible using information from the reading passage and the lecture. The question does **not** ask you to express your personal opinion. You will be able to see the reading passage again when it is time for you to write. You may use your notes to help you answer the question.

Typically, an effective response will be 150 to 225 words long. Your response will be judged on the quality of your writing and on the completeness and accuracy of the content. If you finish your response before time is up, you may click on **NEXT** to go on to the second writing task.

Now you will see the reading passage for 3 minutes. Remember it will be available to you again when you are writing. Immediately after the reading time ends, the lecture will begin, so keep your headset on until the lecture is over.

In the Andes Mountains of Peru are the ruins of numerous ancient structures that have the appearance of military fortifications. The exact purpose of these places is actually a matter of debate for archaeologists. While some believe they were forts used in various armed conflicts, others have concluded that the structures were not designed as defensive bases and were not involved in wars but instead had ceremonial or religious functions. The latter interpretation is much more likely.

To begin with, most of these sites did not have defensive measures which would have enabled them to be effective tools in warfare. For instance, a number of the sites lacked walls that entirely surrounded the interior buildings. Without this integral defensive structure, the forts would have been easily overtaken by attackers. There is simply no way that their builders would have overlooked this weakness if the primary purpose of the forts was to protect their occupants from invaders.

An additional problem is that most of the forts had poor defenses. For instance, many walls lacked parapets. A parapet is a short wall on top of a main wall and is designed to provide protection for defenders standing on top of the main wall. Other sites had walls that provided easy access points for attackers. For instance, some forts had walls with multiple doorways, which would have given determined attackers numerous entry points to the forts.

Lastly, many sites were situated in poor locations as they were far from populated villages and were therefore ill-suited to serve as refuges from attackers for the local populace. They also had no internal sources of water such as wells. Without a secure water source, any fort is doomed to fall once attackers begin besieging it. On account of these weaknesses, these structures could not have had a military purpose.

AT11-01

Directions You have 20 minutes to plan and write your response. Your response will be judged on the basis of the quality of your writing and on how well your response presents the points in the lecture and their relationship to the passage. Typically, an effective response will be 150-225 words.

Question Summarize the points made in the lecture, being sure to specifically explain how they answer the problems raised in the reading passage.

COPY   CUT   PASTE   Word Count : 0

In the Andes Mountains of Peru are the ruins of numerous ancient structures that have the appearance of military fortifications. The exact purpose of these places is actually a matter of debate for archaeologists. While some believe they were forts used in various armed conflicts, other have concluded that the structures were not designed as defensive bases and were not involved in wars but instead had ceremonial or religious functions. The latter interpretation is much more likely.

To begin with, most of these sites did not have defensive measures which would have enabled them to be effective tools in warfare. For instance, a number of the sites lacked walls that entirely surrounded the interior buildings. Without this integral defensive structure, the forts would have been easily overtaken by attackers. There is simply no way that their builders would have overlooked this weakness if the primary purpose of the forts was to protect their occupants from invaders.

An additional problem is that most of the forts had poor defenses. For instance, many walls lacked parapets. A parapet is a short wall on top of a main wall and is designed to provide protection for defenders standing on top of the main wall. Other sites had walls that provided easy access points for attackers. For instance, some forts had walls with multiple doorways, which would have given determined attackers numerous entry points to the forts.

Lastly, many sites were situated in poor locations as they were far from populated villages and were therefore ill-suited to serve as refuges from attackers for the local populace. They also had no internal sources of water such as wells. Without a secure water source, any fort is doomed to fall once attackers begin besieging it. On account of these weaknesses, these structures could not have had a military purpose.

COPY CUT PASTE

Word Count : 0

Writing Based on Knowledge and Experience

For this task, you will write an essay in response to a question that asks you to state, explain, and support your opinion on an issue. You have **30 minutes** to write your essay.

Typically, an effective essay will contain a minimum of 300 words. Your essay will be judged on the quality of your writing. This includes the development of your ideas, the organization of the content, and the quality and accuracy of the language you used to express ideas.

Click on **CONTINUE** to go on.

COPY CUT PASTE

Word Count : 0

Directions Read the question below. You have 30 minutes to plan, write, and revise your essay. Typically, an effective response will contain a minimum of 300 words.

Question

When people are buying something important, such as an automobile or a computer, which of the following should they take into consideration: advice from their friends, advice from the seller, information from the media, or their own opinions? Use specific reasons and examples to support your answer.

Be sure to use your own words. Do not use memorized examples.

COPY CUT PASTE

Word Count : 0

Actual Test

12

Writing Section Directions

 Make sure your headset is on.

This section measures your ability to use writing to communicate in an academic environment. There will be two writing tasks.

For the first writing task, you will read a passage and listen to a lecture and then answer a question based on what you have read and heard. For the second writing task, you will answer a question based on your own knowledge and experience.

Now listen to the directions for the first writing task.

Writing Based on Reading and Listening

For this task, you will first have **3 minutes** to read a passage about an academic topic. You may take notes on the passage if you wish. The passage will then be removed and you will listen to a lecture about the same topic. While you listen, you may also take notes.

Then you will have **20 minutes** to write a response to a question that asks you about the relationship between the lecture you heard and the reading passage. Try to answer the question as completely as possible using information from the reading passage and the lecture. The question does **not** ask you to express your personal opinion. You will be able to see the reading passage again when it is time for you to write. You may use your notes to help you answer the question.

Typically, an effective response will be 150 to 225 words long. Your response will be judged on the quality of your writing and on the completeness and accuracy of the content. If you finish your response before time is up, you may click on **NEXT** to go on to the second writing task.

Now you will see the reading passage for 3 minutes. Remember it will be available to you again when you are writing. Immediately after the reading time ends, the lecture will begin, so keep your headset on until the lecture is over.

The vast majority of children in the United States attend public schools and study in a classroom setting. Yet the homeschooling movement is gaining more and more adherents every year, so there are currently roughly two million American children who do not attend schools but are instead taught at home by either one or both of their parents. These parents are seldom certified as teachers but still excel at educating their children. In fact, homeschooling has several advantages over the learning that takes place at public schools.

The primary benefit is that homeschooled children receive much better educations than students at public schools get. Statistics show that, on average, homeschooled children are much stronger academically than public school children are. In addition, a greater percentage of homeschooled children both complete high school and go on to attend university. While they are at their universities, homeschooled students continue to outperform those students who attended public elementary, middle, and high schools.

Homeschooling also provides social advantages for children. It brings parents and their children closer together since they spend much more time with one another. Homeschooled children additionally do not have to deal with bullying, which is a major issue at many public schools and which has many negative long-term consequences for children who suffer from it. Nor do homeschooled children have to be concerned with the violent students and unmotivated teachers that characterize so many modern-day public schools.

A final benefit is that homeschooled children rarely exhibit any behavioral issues and are proven to be much better at social interactions than public school children are. Many homeschooled children take part in a large number of after-school activities, where they interact with both children and adults. This results in them learning how to behave properly in a variety of settings.

AT12-01

Directions You have 20 minutes to plan and write your response. Your response will be judged on the basis of the quality of your writing and on how well your response presents the points in the lecture and their relationship to the passage. Typically, an effective response will be 150-225 words.

Question Summarize the points made in the lecture, being sure to explain how they challenge specific claims made in the reading passage.

COPY   CUT   PASTE   Word Count : 0

The vast majority of children in the United States attend public schools and study in a classroom setting. Yet the homeschooling movement is gaining more and more adherents every year, so there are currently roughly two million American children who do not attend schools but are instead taught at home by either one or both of their parents. These parents are seldom certified as teachers but still excel at educating their children. In fact, homeschooling has several advantages over the learning that takes place at public schools.

The primary benefit is that homeschooled children receive much better educations than students at public schools get. Statistics show that, on average, homeschooled children are much stronger academically than public school children are. In addition, a greater percentage of homeschooled children both complete high school and go on to attend university. While they are at their universities, homeschooled students continue to outperform those students who attended public elementary, middle, and high schools.

Homeschooling also provides social advantages for children. It brings parents and their children closer together since they spend much more time with one another. Homeschooled children additionally do not have to deal with bullying, which is a major issue at many public schools and which has many negative long-term consequences for children who suffer from it. Nor do homeschooled children have to be concerned with the violent students and unmotivated teachers that characterize so many modern-day public schools.

A final benefit is that homeschooled children rarely exhibit any behavioral issues and are proven to be much better at social interactions than public school children are. Many homeschooled children take part in a large number of after-school activities, where they interact with both children and adults. This results in them learning how to behave properly in a variety of settings.

Writing Based on Knowledge and Experience

For this task, you will write an essay in response to a question that asks you to state, explain, and support your opinion on an issue. You have **30 minutes** to write your essay.

Typically, an effective essay will contain a minimum of 300 words. Your essay will be judged on the quality of your writing. This includes the development of your ideas, the organization of the content, and the quality and accuracy of the language you used to express ideas.

Click on **CONTINUE** to go on.

COPY   CUT   PASTE   Word Count : 0

Directions Read the question below. You have 30 minutes to plan, write, and revise your essay. Typically, an effective response will contain a minimum of 300 words.

Question

Do you agree or disagree with the following statement?

Because modern life is very complex, it is essential for young people to have the ability to plan and organize.

Use specific reasons and examples to support your answer.

Be sure to use your own words. Do not use memorized examples.

COPY CUT PASTE

Word Count : 0

Actual Test

13

Writing Section Directions

 Make sure your headset is on.

This section measures your ability to use writing to communicate in an academic environment. There will be two writing tasks.

For the first writing task, you will read a passage and listen to a lecture and then answer a question based on what you have read and heard. For the second writing task, you will answer a question based on your own knowledge and experience.

Now listen to the directions for the first writing task.

Writing Based on Reading and Listening

For this task, you will first have **3 minutes** to read a passage about an academic topic. You may take notes on the passage if you wish. The passage will then be removed and you will listen to a lecture about the same topic. While you listen, you may also take notes.

Then you will have **20 minutes** to write a response to a question that asks you about the relationship between the lecture you heard and the reading passage. Try to answer the question as completely as possible using information from the reading passage and the lecture. The question does **not** ask you to express your personal opinion. You will be able to see the reading passage again when it is time for you to write. You may use your notes to help you answer the question.

Typically, an effective response will be 150 to 225 words long. Your response will be judged on the quality of your writing and on the completeness and accuracy of the content. If you finish your response before time is up, you may click on **NEXT** to go on to the second writing task.

Now you will see the reading passage for 3 minutes. Remember it will be available to you again when you are writing. Immediately after the reading time ends, the lecture will begin, so keep your headset on until the lecture is over.

One strange natural phenomenon is that large marine mammals such as whales and dolphins occasionally beach themselves. They swim into water so shallow that they cannot return to the open ocean and therefore get trapped. In many cases, these animals cannot be saved, so they die in great numbers. While scientists are not sure precisely why whales and dolphins beach themselves, they have a couple of theories regarding the matter.

One leading possibility is that the mammals, for various reasons, head into shallow water. In some cases, they are following schools of fish to feed, and in other cases, the leader of a pod of whales or dolphins may become ill and thus swims into shallow water to die. The other members of the pod unwittingly follow the leader and find themselves in shallow water, too. When the tide goes out, the whales and dolphins become stranded on the seabed. When the tide comes back in, the animals are too weakened to swim into deeper water and wind up getting washed ashore and die.

Another theory which is gaining adherents is that the sonar used by naval ships damages the whales' and dolphins' brains and internal navigation systems. Both animals use a navigation system similar to sonar as they send out sound waves that bounce back to their brains, which allows them to navigate. Naval sonar waves are so powerful that when they hit these animals, they can cause damage. This was proved in the Bahamas in the year 2000 after a large American naval exercise was held. Soon afterward, there were no fewer than four incidents of whales beaching themselves. Close examinations of the whales showed they had suffered damage to their brains and internal organs, which almost surely hindered their ability to navigate.

AT13-01

Directions You have 20 minutes to plan and write your response. Your response will be judged on the basis of the quality of your writing and on how well your response presents the points in the lecture and their relationship to the passage. Typically, an effective response will be 150-225 words.

Question Summarize the points made in the lecture, being sure to explain how they cast doubt on specific points made in the reading passage.

COPY · CUT · PASTE · Word Count : 0

One strange natural phenomenon is that large marine mammals such as whales and dolphins occasionally beach themselves. They swim into water so shallow that they cannot return to the open ocean and therefore get trapped. In many cases, these animals cannot be saved, so they die in great numbers. While scientists are not sure precisely why whales and dolphins beach themselves, they have a couple of theories regarding the matter.

One leading possibility is that the mammals, for various reasons, head into shallow water. In some cases, they are following schools of fish to feed, and in other cases, the leader of a pod of whales or dolphins may become ill and thus swims into shallow water to die. The other members of the pod unwittingly follow the leader and find themselves in shallow water, too. When the tide goes out, the whales and dolphins become stranded on the seabed. When the tide comes back in, the animals are too weakened to swim into deeper water and wind up getting washed ashore and die.

Another theory which is gaining adherents is that the sonar used by naval ships damages the whales' and dolphins' brains and internal navigation systems. Both animals use a navigation system similar to sonar as they send out sound waves that bounce back to their brains, which allows them to navigate. Naval sonar waves are so powerful that when they hit these animals, they can cause damage. This was proved in the Bahamas in the year 2000 after a large American naval exercise was held. Soon afterward, there were no fewer than four incidents of whales beaching themselves. Close examinations of the whales showed they had suffered damage to their brains and internal organs, which almost surely hindered their ability to navigate.

Writing Based on Knowledge and Experience

For this task, you will write an essay in response to a question that asks you to state, explain, and support your opinion on an issue. You have **30 minutes** to write your essay.

Typically, an effective essay will contain a minimum of 300 words. Your essay will be judged on the quality of your writing. This includes the development of your ideas, the organization of the content, and the quality and accuracy of the language you used to express ideas.

Click on **CONTINUE** to go on.

COPY   CUT   PASTE   Word Count : 0

Directions Read the question below. You have 30 minutes to plan, write, and revise your essay. Typically, an effective response will contain a minimum of 300 words.

Question

Do you agree or disagree with the following statement?

High school students should be strongly encouraged by their parents to find part-time jobs during their summer vacations.

Use specific reasons and examples to support your answer.

Be sure to use your own words. Do not use memorized examples.

COPY　CUT　PASTE

Word Count : 0

Actual Test

14

Writing Section Directions

 Make sure your headset is on.

This section measures your ability to use writing to communicate in an academic environment. There will be two writing tasks.

For the first writing task, you will read a passage and listen to a lecture and then answer a question based on what you have read and heard. For the second writing task, you will answer a question based on your own knowledge and experience.

Now listen to the directions for the first writing task.

Writing Based on Reading and Listening

For this task, you will first have **3 minutes** to read a passage about an academic topic. You may take notes on the passage if you wish. The passage will then be removed and you will listen to a lecture about the same topic. While you listen, you may also take notes.

Then you will have **20 minutes** to write a response to a question that asks you about the relationship between the lecture you heard and the reading passage. Try to answer the question as completely as possible using information from the reading passage and the lecture. The question does **not** ask you to express your personal opinion. You will be able to see the reading passage again when it is time for you to write. You may use your notes to help you answer the question.

Typically, an effective response will be 150 to 225 words long. Your response will be judged on the quality of your writing and on the completeness and accuracy of the content. If you finish your response before time is up, you may click on **NEXT** to go on to the second writing task.

Now you will see the reading passage for 3 minutes. Remember it will be available to you again when you are writing. Immediately after the reading time ends, the lecture will begin, so keep your headset on until the lecture is over.

Agriculture is the mainstay of the food supply in the United States. To maintain the profitability of American farms, to control prices, and to limit the sizes of certain crops, the federal government pays subsidies to numerous farmers. This is done primarily by paying farmers not to grow crops and by insuring them against the loss of crops due to inclement weather and pests. These subsidies provide several advantages for both farmers and the country as a whole.

The primary benefit is that subsidies provide stability for American farmers by permitting them to overcome bad harvests or damage caused by weather or pests and therefore let them avoid going bankrupt. Furthermore, subsidies enable American farmers to invest in new equipment and to try new techniques aimed at increasing production. This stability also serves as an incentive for farmers' children to become farmers themselves when they grow older.

A second advantage of subsidies is that they help stabilize food prices. By paying farmers not to grow too many crops, the government ensures that there is no glut on the market that would cause prices to plummet. Additionally, if farmers could not depend on subsidies to overcome years with poor harvests, then they would have to charge higher prices for their crops to provide insurance for themselves in case of future failures. Accordingly, customers would be obliged to pay higher prices for food.

Finally, subsidies permit American farmers to compete worldwide. Thanks to stable prices, American foodstuffs are sold overseas. In many nations, farming is less expensive than in the United States, so the prices of various items tend to be low. Without subsidies, American farmers would have to charge higher prices, so their crops would not be competitive overseas, and they would sell much fewer crops than they presently do.

Directions You have 20 minutes to plan and write your response. Your response will be judged on the basis of the quality of your writing and on how well your response presents the points in the lecture and their relationship to the passage. Typically, an effective response will be 150-225 words.

Question Summarize the points made in the lecture, being sure to explain how they challenge specific claims made in the reading passage.

Agriculture is the mainstay of the food supply in the United States. To maintain the profitability of American farms, to control prices, and to limit the sizes of certain crops, the federal government pays subsidies to numerous farmers. This is done primarily by paying farmers not to grow crops and by insuring them against the loss of crops due to inclement weather and pests. These subsidies provide several advantages for both farmers and the country as a whole.

The primary benefit is that subsidies provide stability for American farmers by permitting them to overcome bad harvests or damage caused by weather or pests and therefore let them avoid going bankrupt. Furthermore, subsidies enable American farmers to invest in new equipment and to try new techniques aimed at increasing production. This stability also serves as an incentive for farmers' children to become farmers themselves when they grow older.

A second advantage of subsidies is that they help stabilize food prices. By paying farmers not to grow too many crops, the government ensures that there is no glut on the market that would cause prices to plummet. Additionally, if farmers could not depend on subsidies to overcome years with poor harvests, then they would have to charge higher prices for their crops to provide insurance for themselves in case of future failures. Accordingly, customers would be obliged to pay higher prices for food.

Finally, subsidies permit American farmers to compete worldwide. Thanks to stable prices, American foodstuffs are sold overseas. In many nations, farming is less expensive than in the United States, so the prices of various items tend to be low. Without subsidies, American farmers would have to charge higher prices, so their crops would not be competitive overseas, and they would sell much fewer crops than they presently do.

COPY   CUT   PASTE

Writing Based on Knowledge and Experience

For this task, you will write an essay in response to a question that asks you to state, explain, and support your opinion on an issue. You have **30 minutes** to write your essay.

Typically, an effective essay will contain a minimum of 300 words. Your essay will be judged on the quality of your writing. This includes the development of your ideas, the organization of the content, and the quality and accuracy of the language you used to express ideas.

Click on **CONTINUE** to go on.

COPY   CUT   PASTE   Word Count : 0

Directions Read the question below. You have 30 minutes to plan, write, and revise your essay. Typically, an effective response will contain a minimum of 300 words.

Question

Do you agree or disagree with the following statement?

One way to reduce air pollution is for the government to raise the price of gas.

Use specific reasons and examples to support your answer.

Be sure to use your own words. Do not use memorized examples.

Actual Test

15

Writing Section Directions

 Make sure your headset is on.

This section measures your ability to use writing to communicate in an academic environment. There will be two writing tasks.

For the first writing task, you will read a passage and listen to a lecture and then answer a question based on what you have read and heard. For the second writing task, you will answer a question based on your own knowledge and experience.

Now listen to the directions for the first writing task.

Writing Based on Reading and Listening

For this task, you will first have **3 minutes** to read a passage about an academic topic. You may take notes on the passage if you wish. The passage will then be removed and you will listen to a lecture about the same topic. While you listen, you may also take notes.

Then you will have **20 minutes** to write a response to a question that asks you about the relationship between the lecture you heard and the reading passage. Try to answer the question as completely as possible using information from the reading passage and the lecture. The question does **not** ask you to express your personal opinion. You will be able to see the reading passage again when it is time for you to write. You may use your notes to help you answer the question.

Typically, an effective response will be 150 to 225 words long. Your response will be judged on the quality of your writing and on the completeness and accuracy of the content. If you finish your response before time is up, you may click on **NEXT** to go on to the second writing task.

Now you will see the reading passage for 3 minutes. Remember it will be available to you again when you are writing. Immediately after the reading time ends, the lecture will begin, so keep your headset on until the lecture is over.

Many modern-day devices, particularly electronics, require rare minerals during the manufacturing process. These rare minerals are frequently found in some of the world's poorer regions. One such place is the Congo, an African country. Coltan, a mineral that can be refined into tantalum, is found there. Tantalum is heat resistant and does not corrode easily, so it is used to make capacitors for high-end electronic devices such as cell phones. As a result, the coltan mines in Eastern Congo are sources of great wealth, but they have a negative effect on the people there.

The reason is that various rebel groups control most of the Eastern Congo. They use the funds raised from the sale of raw coltan and other minerals to purchase arms and supplies needed to oppose the legitimate government of the Congo. In short, the coltan used by manufacturers around the world is supporting bloodshed in the Congo. To stop this, the world's governments should ban the purchase and importing of Congolese coltan. They should additionally ban the sale of tantalum from nations such as China, where Congolese coltan is smelted in great amounts. This would help dry up the rebels' money source and could help end the rebellion in the Congo.

Because coltan is available from many other regions, it does not have to be bought from the Congo. Australia, Canada, and Brazil all have larger coltan reserves than the Congo. New sources of the mineral in Venezuela and Columbia were discovered recently, too. The world's reserves of coltan outside Africa are nearly three times as great, so they are more than sufficient to supply the growing demand for it. By acquiring coltan from more stable suppliers, the need for the Congo's rebel-controlled coltan will disappear, and the terrible conflict there can finally be halted.

AT15-01

Directions You have 20 minutes to plan and write your response. Your response will be judged on the basis of the quality of your writing and on how well your response presents the points in the lecture and their relationship to the passage. Typically, an effective response will be 150-225 words.

Question Summarize the points made in the lecture, being sure to explain how they challenge specific arguments made in the reading passage.

COPY   CUT   PASTE   Word Count : 0

Many modern-day devices, particularly electronics, require rare minerals during the manufacturing process. These rare minerals are frequently found in some of the world's poorer regions. One such place is the Congo, an African country. Coltan, a mineral that can be refined into tantalum, is found there. Tantalum is heat resistant and does not corrode easily, so it is used to make capacitors for high-end electronic devices such as cell phones. As a result, the coltan mines in Eastern Congo are sources of great wealth, but they have a negative effect on the people there.

The reason is that various rebel groups control most of the Eastern Congo. They use the funds raised from the sale of raw coltan and other minerals to purchase arms and supplies needed to oppose the legitimate government of the Congo. In short, the coltan used by manufacturers around the world is supporting bloodshed in the Congo. To stop this, the world's governments should ban the purchase and importing of Congolese coltan. They should additionally ban the sale of tantalum from nations such as China, where Congolese coltan is smelted in great amounts. This would help dry up the rebels' money source and could help end the rebellion in the Congo.

Because coltan is available from many other regions, it does not have to be bought from the Congo. Australia, Canada, and Brazil all have larger coltan reserves than the Congo. New sources of the mineral in Venezuela and Columbia were discovered recently, too. The world's reserves of coltan outside Africa are nearly three times as great, so they are more than sufficient to supply the growing demand for it. By acquiring coltan from more stable suppliers, the need for the Congo's rebel-controlled coltan will disappear, and the terrible conflict there can finally be halted.

COPY   CUT   PASTE

Word Count : 0

Writing Based on Knowledge and Experience

For this task, you will write an essay in response to a question that asks you to state, explain, and support your opinion on an issue. You have **30 minutes** to write your essay.

Typically, an effective essay will contain a minimum of 300 words. Your essay will be judged on the quality of your writing. This includes the development of your ideas, the organization of the content, and the quality and accuracy of the language you used to express ideas.

Click on **CONTINUE** to go on.

COPY CUT PASTE Word Count : 0

Directions Read the question below. You have 30 minutes to plan, write, and revise your essay. Typically, an effective response will contain a minimum of 300 words.

Question

Do you agree or disagree with the following statement?

Young people today are more likely to devote time and effort to helping others than young people in the past were.

Use specific reasons and examples to support your answer.

Be sure to use your own words. Do not use memorized examples.

COPY   CUT   PASTE

Word Count : 0

Memo

AUTHORS

Michael A. Putlack
- MA in History, Tufts University, Medford, MA, USA
- Expert test developer of TOEFL, TOEIC, and TEPS
- Main author of the Darakwon *How to Master Skills for the TOEFL® iBT* series and *TOEFL® MAP* series

Stephen Poirier
- Candidate for PhD in History, University of Western Ontario, Canada
- Certificate of Professional Technical Writing, Carleton University, Canada
- Co-author of the Darakwon *How to Master Skills for the TOEFL® iBT* series and *TOEFL® MAP* series

Decoding the **TOEFL**® iBT
Actual Test **WRITING** 2 — NEW TOEFL® EDITION

Publisher Chung Kyudo
Editors Kim Minju, Seo Jeongah
Authors Michael A. Putlack, Stephen Poirier
Proofreader Michael A. Putlack
Designers Koo Soojung, Park Sunyoung

First published in December 2019
By Darakwon, Inc.
Darakwon Bldg., 211, Munbal-ro, Paju-si, Gyeonggi-do 10881
Republic of Korea
Tel: 82-2-736-2031 (Ext. 250)
Fax: 82-2-732-2037

Price ₩16,000
ISBN 978-89-277-0870-4 14740
     978-89-277-0862-9 14740 (set)

www.darakwon.co.kr

Components Test Book / Answer Book
8 7 6 5 4 3 2   21 22 23 24 25

Decoding the TOEFL® iBT

Scripts & Sample Answers
Actual Test

WRITING 2

Decoding the TOEFL® iBT

Actual Test

WRITING 2

Scripts & Sample Answers

Actual Test 01

TASK 1 Integrated Writing p. 11

Listening Script

Now listen to part of a lecture on the topic you just read about.

M Professor: The government has once again passed a bill extending the Essential Air Service. For those of you who don't know, the EAS, as it's known, is a program that came into effect in 1978 after airline deregulation occurred. It subsidizes airlines to fly to communities in remote areas such as in Alaska and rural regions more than 110 kilometers from major airports. Unfortunately, this service is costing taxpayers up to 200 million dollars each year and isn't even necessary.

The EAS is supposed to provide air service to places far from large cities, but many airports that benefit from it are barely outside the 110-kilometer limit. That's hardly, uh, remote. The people on these flights frequently take connecting flights at the larger airports they go to. But in many cases, these larger airports are only an hour or so away by car. Most people benefitting from the EAS could simply drive to the larger airport and save themselves the trouble of taking a short commuter flight.

The EAS was originally supposed to cost taxpayers no more than $200 per passenger, but, um, due to rising costs, the government now pays airlines more than $2,000 on some routes. Many of the airplanes used on these routes aren't even half full each flight, which, um, which further drives up the cost per passenger. You know, uh, I couldn't care less if it saves people in rural areas large amounts of money. We should let the market decide what the prices of tickets from these places should be.

And don't be fooled by talk about rural airports providing jobs and economic benefits to their communities. Most of these airports are so small that they provide few jobs and virtually no services. If the EAS ended today, almost nobody would notice.

Sample Answer

Reading Note

EAS provides benefits to people in rural areas

1 **pays airlines to fly commuter aircraft**
   – fly 2-4 times daily
   – operates at 160+ airports
   – airports = 110km away from major airports

2 **passengers pay affordable prices**
   – subsidies → airlines charge lower rates
   – was $200/ticket → has increased lately

3 **improves economies of secluded communities**
   – provides employment at airports
   – flying lessons at many airports

Listening Note

EAS is costly and unnecessary

1 **most airports are not remote**
   – are barely outside 110km limit
   – passengers could drive to larger airports 1 hour away

2 **subsidies have increased in price**
   – paid $2,000/seat on some flights
   – many planes aren't half full
   – should let market determine prices

3 **don't provide benefits to communities**
   – small airports = few jobs + virtually no services
   – few would notice if EAS ended

Sample Essay

The professor lectures against the Essential Air Service (EAS) in his talk and provides three specific claims that challenge the arguments that are made in the reading passage.

To begin with, the professor points out that the EAS was supposed to serve people who live in remote communities. However, he states that most of the airports with flights which are subsidized by the EAS are within an hour's drive of large airports, so people could simply drive to the airports in those cities instead of flying to them. His argument therefore refutes the one in the reading passage that many rural airports are very far from larger cities.

The professor also points out that the airlines are getting paid up to $2,000 per seat on these flights, many of which are less than fifty percent full. In stating that he does not care how much people in rural areas have to pay for plane tickets, he goes against the reading passage. It notes that the subsidies let airlines charge cheaper prices to passengers flying from these airports.

Last, the professor refutes the claim in the reading passage that the EAS provides economic benefits and jobs by subsidizing flights to rural airports. According to him, rural airports hire few people and provide almost no economic benefits to their regions.

Agree

spend too much $ buying pets

– spend hundreds or thousands of $
– e.g. friend bought poodle = $500 → could have visited animal shelter

spend too much $ on accessories

– can buy many items for pets → unnecessary & overpriced
– e.g. sis buys clothes for dog → waste of $

spend too much $ on medical care

– care for animals is better → can treat diseases now
– surgeries are expensive → could use $ in other ways

Sample Essay

I strongly believe that people spend too much money on their pets these days. I have seen numerous instances of people wasting their money when they could have been spending it in other much more productive ways.

First of all, when people buy pets, they often spend a great amount of money. This is particularly true if they purchase the animals from pet stores or breeders. When people get purebred dogs and cats, they frequently spend hundreds or even thousands of dollars. For instance, my best friend's family recently bought a new poodle. It cost his parents around 500 dollars to buy it from a pet store. That is way too much money, especially since they could have visited an animal shelter and spent just a few dollars to get a great animal.

Once people buy pets, they tend to spend too much money on accessories for their animals. Online pet supply stores have pages and pages of items for pets that they sell. Owners can buy special beds, clothes, snacks, and other things for their animals. But almost all of these accessories are totally unnecessary and extremely overpriced. My sister is constantly buying clothes to put on her pet Yorkshire terrier. She thinks it looks cute, but I think it is a waste of money.

Lastly, it is common for people to spend enormous amounts of money on medical care for their pets. In the past, medical treatment for animals was rather poor, but it has improved a great deal in modern times. Doctors can therefore perform all kinds of operations on animals and even treat them for cancer and other diseases. While this means that many animals can live longer lives, the costs of these surgeries are enormous. People could definitely use the money they spend on these operations

in other more beneficial ways.

I love animals a great deal, but I believe a large number of people are wasting their money on their pets. From buying pets to getting accessories for them to paying for operations for their pets, people are spending excessive amounts of money on their animals. They should definitely take that money and spend it in other ways.

Disagree

pets = family members

– e.g. cousin has cat → loves cat → spends lots of $ on it
– not a waste in her opinion

assume responsibility for pet when buy it

– my family's dog was often sick → paid for best care
– must value pets' lives and treat w/dignity

people should spend $ however they want

– people value different things
– if want to spend $ on pet, is okay
– e.g. aunt has 2 cats → gets pleasure from spending $ on them

Sample Essay

It may appear that some people are spending large amounts of money on their pets and that they could use their money in other ways. However, in my opinion, there is nothing wrong with people spending hundreds or thousands of dollars on their pets.

To begin with, nowadays, many people treat their pets as if they were members of their own families. As an example, my cousin has a cat that she adores. When she is at home, she and her cat are almost always together. She loves her cat very much, so I see no problem with her spending money to purchase accessories, toys, and snacks for it. In my cousin's mind, she is not wasting her money but is instead spending her money on something she loves.

Next, when you purchase a pet, you assume responsibility for it. You therefore need to provide it with what it needs to live comfortably. This includes spending money if it needs an expensive medical procedure. Several years ago, my family owned a golden retriever. He got sick a lot, and we did not have much money, but my parents always took him to the veterinarian and paid for him to get the best possible care. They taught us that we should value the lives of our pets and treat them with dignity no matter what the price.

Last, I am a great believer in letting people spend their money however they want. No two people value the same things equally. What I feel is important may be something of no interest to another person. Therefore, if people want to spend huge sums of money on their pets, why should I tell them not to? It is likely that their pets mean a great deal to them. It definitely brings my aunt great pleasure to spend money on her two cats. Since she enjoys using her money on them, I think she should continue to do so.

I do not believe that people waste their money on their pets. People love their pets and are responsible for them, so it is only natural to spend money on them. In addition, people are free to use their money however they like. If they happen to like spending money on their pets, then they are welcome to do so.

Actual Test 02

TASK 1 Integrated Writing

p. 21

Listening Script

Now listen to part of a lecture on the topic you just read about.

W Professor: The term used to describe plants that close their leaves at night is nyctinasty. The mechanism causing this action is a biochemical reaction at the base of each leaf, which forces it to shut. The initiators of this movement are the coming of darkness and the dropping of the ambient temperature. Botanists know how the mechanism works, but, uh, well, we don't know why plants do this. Unfortunately, every single one of the major theories regarding this behavior has problems.

Many botanists theorize that plants close their leaves to make more efficient use of water. But let's keep in mind that some aquatic plants close their leaves at night, and, well, they never lack water, do they? In addition, I don't believe the closing of leaves reduces the amount of water and therefore makes the growth of fungi less likely to occur. Why don't I believe this . . . ? Simple. If this behavior were really effective at preventing fungi from growing, then more plants would have evolved so that their leaves close at night.

Charles Darwin . . . yeah, the evolutionist . . . uh, he hypothesized that this action helped keep plants warm at night. But you should know that many plants which close their leaves grow in warm climates and thrive in summertime, so freezing isn't a relevant issue for them. Finally, some speculate that the closing of leaves lets predators such as, uh, owls, hunt prey more easily. Hmm . . . It sounds interesting, but there's no hard evidence supporting this theory. You see, uh, there's not a single long-term study comparing the survival rates of nyctinastic plants and non-nyctinastic plants when they both grow in areas with nocturnal plant eaters. So, uh, while this concept may sound interesting, it's pure speculation with not a single shred of evidence available to back it up.

Sample Answer

Reading Note

3 theories on why plants close their leaves at night

1 lets water flow to other plant parts
    – can go to stems and roots → needed there
    – prevents moisture from accumulating on leaves
    – can inhibit growth of fungi on leaves

2 **avoid freezing temperatures**
    – thought of Charles Darwin
    – reduce surface area of leaves exposed to weather
    – keeps leaves from being harmed

3 **aids predators**
    – can find prey more easily
    – prey = eat leaves of plants
    – by killing prey, predators are helping plants

Listening Note

Theories on nyctinasty have problems

1 **not because of water**
    – some aquatic plants close leaves → don't need water
    – doesn't make fungi growth less likely → if was effective, more plants would do it

2 **not because of weather**
    – many plants grow in warm weather in summer
    – freezing isn't an issue

3 **not to help predators**
    – no evidence to support
    – no long-term studies on survival rates of nyctinastic vs. non-nyctinastic plants

Sample Essay

The topic of the professor's lecture is nyctinastic plants and the reasons they close their leaves at night. The professor's lecture casts doubt on the three possible explanations for this behavior that are provided in the reading passage.

She begins by covering the notion that the plants fold their leaves to use water more efficiently. The reading passage declares that the folding of leaves lets water get to the plant parts that need and prevents fungi from growing, too. The professor doubts this since the leaves of some water plants close at night, and those plants never lack water. She also disputes the claim about fungi because she believes more plants would have evolved to having folding leaves if it really were an effective method.

Next, the professor covers the theory proposed by Charles Darwin. He thought plants closed their leaves to keep from freezing at night. But she remarks that many plants with folding leaves grow in summer in warm climates, so they never experience cold weather.

The third theory involves speculation that the leaves fold to enable predators to identify prey more easily. The prey is usually animals that eat the leaves of nyctinastic plants. The professor counters this idea by saying that there are no studies providing evidence this is true, so it is merely a matter of speculation.

TASK 2 Independent Writing p. 26

Sample Answer 1

Regular Field Trips

get hands-on learning

– went to automobile manufacturing plant
– assembly line → saw how cars made
– can't duplicate experience in classroom

see practical value of knowledge learned at school

– find history boring
– went to war memorial → understood need to learn history
– study harder in history class now

can be inspired

– went to animation studio → best friend uninterested in school but loved studio
– pays closer attention at school now

Sample Essay

There are many people who believe students should only be taught in the classroom, but I am not one of them. Instead, in my opinion, going on regular field trips is an ideal way for schools to educate students. There are three reasons that I feel this way.

Firstly, students can get hands-on learning by visiting various places on field trips. My school takes students on several field trips each year. I love going on them

because we get to visit places where I can learn. For instance, there is a large automobile manufacturing plant near my school, and we went on a field trip there this year. We got to go down on the assembly line to see exactly how cars are made. That was a learning experience which is simply impossible to duplicate while studying in a classroom.

Secondly, by going on field trips, it is possible for students to see the practical value of the knowledge we learn at school. I often find history boring, and I dislike memorizing all of the names, dates, and places that my history teacher lectures us about. But when my class visited a war memorial on a recent field trip, I started understanding the need to learn this information. When I noticed how many people had died at that battle, I realized I had to know about my country's history, so I made up my mind to study harder in history class.

Thirdly, lots of students get inspired when they go on field trips, so they begin to study harder at school. One month ago, my class visited an animation studio, and we saw how animated movies are made. One of my best friends had previously been uninterested in school, but she was fascinated by the studio. Since that trip, she has paid closer attention at school, especially in her art and math classes. She now realizes she has to work harder at school to be successful in life.

Schools should definitely take students on regular field trips. The students can get hands-on learning, they can see how useful the information they learn at school is, and they can be inspired to learn more after visiting some places. Those are three good reasons for students to go on as many field trips as possible.

Sample Answer 2

Learning in Classrooms

can learn more in classrooms

– field trips = no learning + focus on a few subjects
– went to art gallery → wasted experience

classrooms → access to educational material

– don't go to museum → go to museum's website
– teacher can lecture class about exhibits

students goof off during field trips

– zoo trip → many students played so didn't learn
– students distracted me → couldn't learn

Sample Essay

While I enjoy going on field trips, I do not believe they are an ideal way to learn. Personally, I support students not going on any field trips but instead getting all of their learning from classrooms.

The first reason I feel this way is that students can learn a wide variety of topics in classrooms. On a typical school day, I study math, science, history, Korean, English, and either art or music. As a result, I receive a broad education in at least six different subjects each day. However, when we go on a field trip, we receive no classroom learning for an entire day, and our trips only focus on one or two subjects. Last month, we took a field trip to an art gallery, but all we did was look at some paintings. The guides failed to tell us about the styles the painters used or anything else educational. Since we did not learn anything there, it was basically a wasted experience.

Another reason I support classroom learning is that classrooms have access to all kinds of educational material. Nowadays, if we want to see an exhibit at a museum, we do not need to visit the museum in person. Instead, we can visit the museum's website from a school computer and view the exhibit online. Simultaneously, our teacher can lecture us about the importance of the items on exhibit, which can increase our knowledge.

A third reason I dislike field trips is that many students just goof off during them, so they do not learn anything at all. When my class visited the city zoo last semester, half of the students just ran around and played. They ignored the tour guide, so they did not learn anything he told us about the animals. Those students additionally distracted me, so I missed out on some valuable information due to their disruptive behavior. I would have learned more if I had gone to the zoo by myself on the weekend.

Even though field trips are fun, students do not always learn much on them, so classrooms are a better place for students to be educated. Therefore, I support students learning in their classrooms and not going on any field trips.

TASK 1 Integrated Writing   p. 31

Listening Script

Now listen to part of a lecture on the topic you just read about.

M Professor: So, uh, clearly both rootworm larvae and adult rootworm beetles are harming corn crops all around the country. Farmers are fighting back though and have found some effective methods to rid themselves of rootworms. Nevertheless, none of the three most preferred methods is one hundred percent effective, so some amount of corn gets lost each year despite the best efforts of farmers.

Crop rotation seems to work well by depriving the rootworm larvae of a food source once they hatch. But, well, rootworms have evolved to counter this method. One type of adult rootworm beetle has the ability to move to other fields, such as those planted with soybeans, where it, uh, where it then lays its eggs. The next year, when corn is rotated in and soybeans are rotated out, the eggs are waiting for the corn. In addition, rootworm eggs can remain in the ground for two seasons before they hatch, so farmers would need to leave their fields empty of corn for more than two years for crop rotation to be totally effective.

Some farmers have met with success by planting corn earlier than normal. But remember that weather is unpredictable, especially in places in northern regions. Many farmers have lost their entire crops when they planted too early in spring. Why . . . ? Well, late frosts and even snowstorms happen in April in some places, and those can easily kill young corn plants.

And, uh, what about insecticides? Well, they're effective, but they're also expensive and require lots of time and labor to apply. The reason is that many insecticides have to be put at the base of each individual plant, which is labor intensive. And some rootworms are developing immunity to certain kinds of insecticides, which is making these poisons completely useless.

Sample Answer

Reading Note

3 effective ways to deal w/rootworms

1 crop rotation
   – grow corn 1 year & leave fields fallow 1 year

– deprives rootworm larvae of food

– die after hatching → no rootworms the next year

2 **plant corn earlier in spring**

– roots bigger when rootworms hatch → less edible

– corn pollinates earlier → adult rootworm beetles lay fewer eggs

3 **use insecticides**

– effective against eggs and larvae

– mass spraying → kills adult rootworm beetles

Listening Note

Methods of killing rootworms aren't 100% effective

1 **rootworms evolved to counter crop rotation**

– move to other fields and lay eggs

– eggs stay in ground for 2 seasons → need to leave fields fallow longer

2 **unpredictable weather**

– can lose entire crops

– late frosts & April snowstorms → kill young corn plants

3 **insecticides have problems**

– expensive + labor intensive

– rootworms becoming immune to some insecticides

Sample Essay

During his lecture, the professor discusses rootworms and the harm they cause the corn plants of American farmers. Although the author of the reading passage believes there are effective ways to defeat rootworms, the professor casts doubt on the usefulness of each method.

The first method the professor believes is ineffective is crop rotation. According to the reading passage, by not planting corn crops in a field for a year, rootworm larvae can be deprived of food and killed. But the professor states that some rootworms move to fields planted with other crops, which makes crop rotation useless. He also claims that some rootworm eggs do not hatch for two years, so a field must remain fallow for a longer period.

The professor then argues against planting corn earlier in spring. The reading passage notes that this can make corn roots bigger and more resistant to attacks by larvae. But the professor says that planting corn too early, particularly in northern regions, makes the corn liable to succumb to bad weather. He declares that April frosts and snowstorms can kill many plants.

Finally, the professor agrees with the reading passage that insecticides are effective at killing rootworms.

However, he points out the great amount of time and expense in using insecticides. He also mentions that some rootworms are becoming immune to the insecticides presently used.

TASK 2 Independent Writing   p. 36

Sample Answer 1

Agree

focus energy & concentration

– have homework in 3-4 subjects

– friends work on all subjects together

– work on one subject → can understand better and get better grades

can complete work quickly

– get home from school → do math homework first = 20-30 minutes

– choose another subject and do work until done = 2-3 hours total

– friends change assignments = 4 or 5 hours total

Sample Essay

I could not possibly agree more with the statement. It is definitely better for a student to complete one homework assignment and then to start another than to work on several assignments at the same time.

The main reason is that by working on a single assignment, you can focus all of your energy and concentration on it. I frequently have homework in three or four subjects after I return home from school each day. Some of my friends do their homework by working for a few minutes on one subject and then doing another project despite not having completed the first assignment. I find that method highly inefficient. What I do is choose a subject and work on it until it is done. When I do that, I think only about that particular subject. As a result, I not only learn the material better, but I also get better grades on my assignments than my friends.

Another reason to work on only one homework assignment at a time is that you can complete your work very quickly. For instance, when I get home from school, I almost always do my math homework first. It takes me around twenty or thirty minutes to complete. Then, I choose another subject and work exclusively on it until I am done. I repeat this process until I finish everything. That usually takes me around two or three hours. On the other hand, I have some friends who do some work on an assignment and then change to another subject before completing it. They are always complaining about having to spend four or five hours a night to finish their homework.

A student should only work on one homework assignment at a time. That will enable the student to use all of his or her energy on that project, which will improve the person's focus. That individual will also experience fewer delays since he or she will be working on just one assignment rather than on multiple ones. It is clear to me that this method is much better than doing multiple assignments at the same time.

Disagree

can be productive

- have trouble w/project → start working on another = more efficient
- e.g. was writing history paper → writer's block → did math problems instead → finished paper later

can get good idea for one assignment while working on another

- has happened several times to friends and me
- e.g. friend was writing essay → thought of idea for science project → started doing it → won second prize in contest

Sample Essay

I disagree with the statement because I am the type of person who prefers to do several homework assignments at once. In fact, I strongly dislike it when I only work on one subject at a time.

For one, I like working on multiple assignments because I find that doing so lets me be extremely productive. The reason is that if I have trouble with one of the assignments I am working on, I can stop doing it and start working on a different one instead. That way, instead of doing nothing at all, I can utilize my time efficiently. Recently, I had to write a history paper and solve some math problems. I started working on the paper, but I got writer's block, so I quit doing it. Then, I began to solve the math problems. Later that night, I went back to finish writing the paper and to solve the remaining math problems. As a result, I completed work on two assignments and did a significant amount of work on another on the same day. I was proud of myself for being so productive.

Another reason I think it is better to work on multiple assignments at once is that a person can get a good idea for one assignment while working on another. This has happened to me several times, and it has also happened to my friends. A while ago, one of my friends was working on an essay for his literature class. While

he was doing his essay, something that he wrote made him start thinking about science. That gave him an idea for the science project he was doing. He stopped writing the essay and began working on the science project. When he completed the science project, he entered it in a contest and won second prize. He never would have had such a great project if he had not gotten inspired while writing his essay.

Clearly, it is better to work on multiple homework assignments at the same time than to work on only a single one. You can be more productive, and you can get great ideas for the other assignments you are working on.

Actual Test 04

TASK 1 Integrated Writing p. 41

Listening Script

Now listen to part of a lecture on the topic you just read about.

W Professor: In the First Book of Kings in the Old Testament of the Bible, you can read the story of how King Solomon sent a large fleet of ships to the wealthy city of Ophir. That's O-P-H-I-R, uh, by the way. When the fleet returned, it had a vast hoard of wealth, including gold, silver, gems, animals, and sandalwood. However, following that voyage, no other fleets sailed for Ophir, and the city's location became lost to history. Modern scholars, however, believe it was located either in Africa or India. I have my doubts about both though.

Some archaeologists have declared that the ruins of an ancient city in Zimbabwe are those of Ophir. Yet those ruins have only been dated to medieval times and not to King Solomon's era. In addition, while gold was mined there in the Middle Ages, there was no gold production in that region in ancient times. Some other archaeologists claim a place on the Ethiopian coast where the Afar people live is where Ophir once was. Yes, Ophir and Afar sound similar, but let's remember that many words in the Bible come from other languages. They were translated into Hebrew and then into Greek. So connecting words according to similarities in their sounds isn't a good way to conduct historical research.

Some believe a place in southern India, which was the

primary source of sandalwood in ancient times, was the site of Ophir. Many archaeologists have proposed various places in India, yet there's no physical evidence at any of these locations. Thus these sites can all be eliminated from contention. It's possible, however, that a natural disaster, such as an earthquake or tsunami, caused Ophir to be submerged beneath the ocean. But more excavating must be done to determine if that theory is correct.

Sample Answer

Reading Note

Ancient city of Ophir → two possible locations

1 somewhere in Africa
   – Zimbabwe → was center of gold production
   – Afar people of Ethiopia → name is similar to Ophir

2 somewhere in India
   – trip took 3 years → may have traveled far
   – many places in India → have names similar to Ophir
   – places in southern India → had gold, ivory, peacocks, and apes
   – southern India → was major source of sandalwood

Listening Note

Ophir → may not have been in Africa or India

1 not in Zimbabwe or Ethiopia
   – gold in Zimbabwe → mined in Middle Ages, not in ancient times
   – Afar and Ophir sound similar → but words were translated from other languages to Hebrew to Greek → not a good way to do historical research

2 not in southern India
   – no physical evidence anywhere
   – perhaps earthquake or tsunami caused Ophir to sink beneath the ocean → need to do more excavating

Sample Essay

The professor discusses the ancient city of Ophir. She mentions that many archaeologists believe it was located either in Africa or India, yet she points out that there are problems with the claims they make.

Regarding Africa, the professor feels that neither Zimbabwe nor Ethiopia was the site of Ophir. The reading passage claims that some ruins in a gold-producing area of Zimbabwe are those of Ophir, but the professor points out that the ruins date back to medieval times. She also says that gold was not mined in that

region during biblical times. While the reading passage mentions similarities between the word Ophir and the Afar people of Ethiopia, the professor remarks that words from the Bible came from many languages and were translated into Hebrew and then into Greek. Thus she believes it is unwise to do historical research based only on names.

As for India, the reading passage stresses that there are places in India with names similar to Ophir and that all of the items the fleet brought back, including sandalwood, could be acquired in southern India. The professor, however, remarks that there is no physical evidence at any of these places. She raises the possibility of Ophir having sunk into the ocean, but she states that there needs to be excavating done to discover its ruins.

TASK 2 Independent Writing   p. 46

Sample Answer 1

Agree

live in globalized age
– many people travel abroad
– e.g. sis went to Europe but didn't know about culture → made several mistakes

people doing business with foreigners
– know about culture → make good impression
– e.g. mother knew about Indian culture → landed contract

many people immigrate to new lands
– may meet foreigners in own country
– e.g. talked to Russian in city → need to know about culture

Sample Essay

I fully support the statement. I believe learning about other cultures is of extreme importance for university students, so I am in favor of making it mandatory for universities to have to teach their students about other cultures.

To begin with, we live in a globalized age when traveling to other lands is simple, fast, and inexpensive. Therefore, large numbers of people visit foreign countries these days. However, many of them know little about the places they go to. My sister traveled to Europe for one month three years ago. Unfortunately, she knew nothing about European culture, so she made several cultural mistakes while she was there. She would have benefitted greatly from some university courses on foreign cultures.

In addition, people are doing business with individuals from foreign countries more than they did in the past. To make a good impression on a business partner, it is ideal to know as much about his or her culture as possible. My mother did business with a client from India recently. She impressed the client with her knowledge of Indian customs and culture, and that had a great deal to do with her landing a contract with that man's firm.

Finally, because so many people immigrate to other nations nowadays, even if a person does not travel abroad, he or she is still likely to encounter foreigners at home. Just the other day while I was walking down the street, a foreigner from Russia stopped and asked me for directions. It was a bit difficult to explain since she did not speak my language well and I do not speak any Russian. Nevertheless, it showed me the importance of knowing about foreign cultures since the chances of meeting foreigners in my city on a daily basis are high.

For those three reasons, I strongly feel that universities should make it required for their students to learn about other cultures. Doing so would help the students avoid making mistakes, let them do business with foreigners more easily, and assist them in dealing with immigrants more effectively.

Sample Answer 2

Disagree

many people never leave home countries
- don't need to learn about other cultures
- is pointless

others uninterested in foreign cultures
- cousin travels abroad often
- package tours → doesn't meet locals
- is boring and useless

students shouldn't have to pay for classes they don't want
- best friend's bro → has to take culture class
- wants to take comp sci class → but can't graduate if no culture class
- unfair + waste of time and $

Sample Essay

At first glance, the statement seems reasonable. However, when I think more about it, I find myself opposing it. I therefore disagree with the statement and believe it should not be mandatory for university students to study other cultures.

For starters, there are many university graduates who never leave their home countries during their entire lives. As a result, they have no need to learn about the customs of tribes in Africa, the cultures of people in

Southeast Asia, or how people in Europe act during certain festivals. For those people, studying other cultures at their universities is pointless.

Another reason is that many people are uninterested in learning about foreign cultures. Universities should not force these individuals to learn something they do not care about. My cousin is a good example of one of those people. He has traveled abroad several times, but he has always gone on package tours, so he rarely interacts with locals. He enjoys visiting places of historical interest as well as museums and galleries, but he has guides who speak his language. He simply does not care to learn about other people's cultures. For him and others like him, a mandatory university class would be a boring and useless experience.

Last of all, universities ought to remember that the students are the ones who are paying to learn, and they should not be obligated to pay for classes they have no desire to take. My best friend's older brother is currently a university student, and he is being forced to take a course on foreign cultures. He hates the class and wants to drop it to register for a computer science class since he is majoring in that subject. But he will not be permitted to graduate unless he completes the culture class. That strikes me as both unfair and a waste of time and money for my friend's brother.

Even though foreign cultures are interesting to many people, nobody should be forced to learn about them at a university. People who will never travel abroad or who are uninterested in other cultures do not need these classes, and some people would prefer to take other classes instead. These individuals should be allowed to avoid culture classes.

Actual Test 05

TASK 1 Integrated Writing

p. 51

Listening Script

Now listen to part of a lecture on the topic you just read about.

M Professor: I must confess that I really dislike traffic cameras. In the past month, I've been given two speeding tickets by those cameras. In each case, I was barely exceeding the speed limit, so a real police officer most likely wouldn't have bothered ticketing me. However, because it was a mindless camera, my car was photographed, and I was sent a fine in the mail on both occasions. You know, um, there are many others who feel the same as me: Traffic cameras are more trouble than they're worth and should be banned.

I did some investigating into traffic cameras, and I discovered a few startling things. For one, a study conducted in the state of Florida in 2012 showed that rear-end collisions at intersections with traffic cameras actually increased. That's right: They happened more often than before. The reason was that drivers were stopping suddenly when the lights changed. That let drivers avoid getting ticketed for running red lights, but, um, the people behind them often failed to stop, so they rammed those cars ahead of them.

An additional problem concerns money. The fines drivers have to pay can be hundreds of dollars per ticket, so traffic cameras raise millions of dollars annually. But that's like an extra tax on people, and nobody got the opportunity to vote on whether or not to approve it. Additionally, many traffic cameras are installed and maintained by companies that keep a percentage of each fine they generate.

Finally, the cameras aren't nearly as accurate as their supporters say they are. Many traffic citations get sent to the wrong people. Recently, in the state of, uh, Louisiana, I believe, this happened . . . A man was fined even though the picture of the speeding car clearly showed it wasn't his vehicle and he wasn't the driver. Unbelievable, huh?

Sample Answer

Reading Note

Automatic traffic camera systems = many advantages

1 require people to obey traffic laws
  – reduced number of traffic accidents
  – high-risk intersections w/cameras → reduction in traffic accidents

2 generate income for cities and states
  – get $ from fines violators pay
  – spend $ to enhance communities
  – e.g. use for libraries & public education

3 accurately record traffic violations
  – photograph license plates, record speeds of vehicles, and take pictures of drivers
  – provide proof drivers broke the law

Listening Note

Traffic cameras should be banned

1 accidents increased due to traffic cameras
  – 2012 survey in Florida
  – rear-end collisions ↑ due to cameras
  – drivers stopped suddenly to avoid tickets → but got rear-ended by others

2 fines are expensive
  – can be hundreds of $ per fine
  – are like a tax nobody voted for

3 aren't accurate
  – citations get sent to wrong people
  – e.g. man was fined → picture of car wasn't his car, and he wasn't driver

Sample Essay

During his lecture, the professor points out several disadvantages of traffic cameras. His reasons for disliking them directly challenge the arguments made in the reading passage, whose author is in favor of the cameras.

The first point the professor makes is that traffic cameras have caused an increase in the number of traffic accidents in some places. He mentions a study that happened in Florida. According to it, the number of accidents increased because cars were getting rear-ended when they stopped suddenly at red lights to avoid getting tickets. This example contradicts the reading passage, which claims that traffic cameras lead to fewer accidents.

The second point made is that the fines people have to pay are like extra taxes that nobody ever voted on. The professor further dislikes that the companies which operate the cameras get to keep some of the fine money. These statements are in contrast to the assertion in the reading passage that cities and states spend the fine money on residents.

The third point the professor makes is that some people get ticketed despite committing no traffic violations. The reading passage makes the claim that traffic cameras are accurate and do not make mistakes, but the professor provides an example of a man being given a ticket for a violation he did not commit.

TASK 2 Independent Writing p. 56

The Quality of Food

shouldn't eat too much fast food

– friends and I love fast food
– is bad for body = low in nutrition but high in calories, sugar, and fat

eat more fruits and vegetables

– sometimes eat fruit → but don't eat enough
– don't like how vegetables taste

cut down on junk food

– love chocolate and ice cream
– am overweight

Sample Essay

If I could change one aspect of my life in order to improve my health, I would opt to alter the quality of the food I eat. There are three main reasons why I would act in this manner.

The first one is that I eat too much fast food, which is well-known for being low in quality. I love the taste of fast food, and so do my friends, so we regularly eat at fast-food restaurants when we hang out together after school or on the weekend. I know fast food is bad for my body because it is generally low in nutrition but high in calories, sugar, and fat, but I have trouble stopping eating it. It would be great if I could change that bad eating habit of mine.

Secondly, I would change my diet so that I consume more fresh fruits and vegetables than I do now. I occasionally eat an apple, banana, or orange, but I do not eat nearly as much fruit as I should. I am also aware that vegetables are healthy foods and provide a great deal of nutritional benefits, but I dislike how most of them taste. Nevertheless, it would improve my health significantly if I ate more of these types of foods.

Last of all, I really need to cut down on the amount of junk food I eat. I love chocolate and ice cream so much that I eat them nearly every day. That has resulted in me being quite a bit overweight. My mother tells me I could lose weight easily and become healthier if I would just cut down on them or eliminate them entirely from my

diet.

I definitely have poor eating habits, so I would change them dramatically if I could to improve my health. I would eat less fast food and junk food, and I would eat more fruits and vegetables. By changing my eating habits in those three ways, I would almost instantly improve my health.

The Amount of Exercise

play sports → get in better shape + have fun

– don't enjoy individual sports
– play team sport → soccer or basketball = fun

reduce stress if exercise

– friends exercise → say feel better after doing it
– exercise → lower stress levels → improved health

lower weight

– should lose a few kg
– bro was obese → started walking → lost 20kg

Sample Essay

I consider myself to be in reasonably good health, but I could become healthier since I am not a very active person. Therefore, of the three options, I would choose to change the amount of exercise I get.

The first way I could improve my health through exercise would be to play some sports with my friends. By playing sports, I could not only get into better shape, but I could also have fun. I do not particularly enjoy playing individual sports though, so I would have to play a team sport such as soccer or basketball. I think it would be fun for me to play a sport even though I do not think I am an athletic person at all.

A second benefit to my health would be that I could reduce my stress level by exercising. While I do not currently exercise that often, some of my friends do. They frequently mention that they feel so much better after playing a sport, jogging, or swimming. While they are doing those activities, they do not think about their school, family, or other problems, so exercise definitely helps lower their stress levels, which then improves their health.

Finally, by exercising, I would be able to lower my weight, which would definitely make me healthier. I should probably lose a few kilograms, and I think exercising is both the easiest and the most fun way to do it. My older brother used to be extremely obese, but he started walking every day around two years ago. The transformation was incredible as he lost more than twenty kilograms in a year. I do not need to lose that much weight, but, if I start walking with my brother, I know my health will improve.

By increasing the amount of exercise I get, I will be able to improve my health a great deal. If I play sports or do a similar activity, I can have fun, get in shape, reduce my stress level, and lose weight. Those are some great reasons to exercise more.

Actual Test 06

TASK 1 Integrated Writing

p. 61

Listening Script

Now listen to part of a lecture on the topic you just read about.

W Professor: The frog is a major part of many ecosystems, but frog populations around the world are in peril. However, preventing the demise of the frog is, uh, problematic for a couple of reasons. First, people don't agree regarding why many frog species have gone extinct lately. Second, saving frogs is going to be a very costly battle.

Many people believe higher temperatures around the globe are causing marshlands, where frogs are typically found, to disappear. This, in turn, is causing the deaths of large numbers of frogs. Okay, um, while it's true that marshlands are disappearing, the problem is that humans are draining them to build houses and other buildings on. There hasn't been any global warming in more than fifteen years, so blaming the weather for killing frogs is wrong.

Now, uh, I totally agree that the chemicals in insecticides and weed killers are harming frogs. However . . . those chemicals are crucial for farmers to grow enough crops to feed everyone. If they didn't use any chemicals, food would become much more expensive . . . uh, and scarce. So do we choose to do what's best for humans and continue using these chemicals? Or do we protect frogs at the risk of higher food prices?

I'm also aware that frogs with diseases are being transported to other countries, where they infect native populations. What's needed is a large-scale screening process for frogs before they're exported. But implementing that would be enormously expensive,

and most countries aren't willing to spend that much money. And let's keep in mind that frogs are vital for some medical research on disease affecting humans, so banning the exporting of frogs won't happen. After all, when it comes down to a choice between saving frogs and saving humans, humans are always going to win.

Sample Answer

Reading Note

Humans are causing frogs to go extinct around the world

1 global warming
   – many believe is caused by humans
   – causing marshland habitats of frogs to disappear

2 chemical pesticides + weed killers
   – seep into groundwater → flows into marshes
   – porous frog skin absorbs chemicals → frogs die

3 frogs transported worldwide
   – rarely tested for diseases
   – chytridiomycosis → has spread far → made up to 100 species go extinct

Listening Note

Not sure why frogs going extinct + saving frogs = expensive

1 no global warming in 15 years
   – isn't reason marshlands are disappearing
   – humans draining them to build houses and buildings on them

2 chemicals are needed by farmers
   – if don't use chemicals, then food becomes expensive and scarce
   – should take care of humans or frogs?

3 large-scale screening process for frogs
   – would be expensive to implement
   – most countries don't want to
   – frogs vital for research → can't ban exporting of them

Sample Essay

The professor's lecture covers the recent extinctions of many species of frogs. She points out that people cannot agree exactly why frogs are going extinct and adds that protecting frogs will be expensive. In those two ways, she challenges the arguments made in the reading passage.

To begin with, the professor rejects the claim in the reading passage that global warming is causing marshlands, where frogs live, to disappear. She says there has been no global warming in a decade and a half, so it is not the reason there are fewer marshlands today. Instead, human development is making marshlands disappear.

Next, the professor points out that it is true, as the reading passage notes, that insecticides and pesticides are causing the deaths of many frogs. But she states that banning them would result in higher prices for food and less food for people around the world.

Lastly, the professor agrees with the reading passage that frogs with diseases are being transported around the world and infecting other populations of frogs. However, she mentions that screening frogs for diseases would be too costly for most countries and that banning the export of frogs will not happen due to their importance, especially for medical research.

TASK 2 Independent Writing

p. 66

Sample Answer 1

Agree

eat meals together → are close
- prepare meals + clean up together
- has made us closer than other families

can talk about problems
- bro talked about problem w/friend → listened and made suggestions
- bro used suggestion → solved problem

can chat about accomplishments and goals
- talked about my math A+ → congratulated me
- sis said wants to go to med school → encouraged her

Sample Essay

I agree with the statement that it is very important for family members to eat together regularly. My family eats together virtually every night, and we have benefitted from this in a number of ways.

First of all, all of the people in my family—my parents, two sisters, brother, and me—are really close to one another. We get along quite well, and I think one of the reasons is that we eat our meals together so often. When it is time to eat, preparing lunch or dinner becomes a team effort. Some of us work in the kitchen to prepare the food while the rest of us set the table. When the meal ends, everybody helps clean off the table, put the leftovers away, and wash the dishes. By working at a team, we have become closer than people in most other families are.

Another reason our family meals are so important is that

we can discuss any problems we are having as we eat. We always make an effort to discuss our lives, especially if something is going badly. Last night, my brother told us about a problem he is having with one of his friends. Everyone listened carefully, and then we made a few suggestions on what he could do. Today, he used one of those suggestions and fixed the problem between him and his friend.

A third reason is that we also use our family meals as opportunities to chat about both our accomplishments and our goals for the future. The other day, I told everyone about the A+ I got on my math test, so my family members all congratulated me. That made me happy. And my sister recently mentioned her desire to attend medical school. We encouraged her to do that, which made her confident she had made the right choice.

It is unfortunate that more families do not often eat their meals together these days. If they were like my family and ate together more often, they would be closer to one another, and they would be able to talk about their problems, accomplishments, and goals as well.

Sample Answer 2

Disagree

rarely eat together → but are close
- busy w/work & school → eat when hungry
- not eating together hasn't affected negatively

don't talk during meals
- talk at other times
- in living room → turned off TV → spoke about lives

everyone in family can cook
- don't need to wait for one person to cook
- if hungry, just make food
- gives family flexibility

Sample Essay

It is great when families take the time to eat their meals together with regularity. However, I do not believe it is very important for them to eat together, so I disagree with the statement.

My family rarely eats meals together. Most weeks, we only have meals together on either Saturday or Sunday night. The reason is that we are all busy either at work or school. Since our schedules are so different, we eat whenever we are hungry. Despite the fact that we do not eat together that much, we are still a close family, and we all get along well with one another. Obviously, the way we eat has not affected us negatively.

Many families enjoy talking during their meals, but my family is not like them. When we eat, we rarely talk. Instead, we have other times when we get together as a complete family and chat about various topics. For instance, last Wednesday night, all of us were in the living room, so we turned off the television and spoke to one another. We did not need to have food to get us to open up and to speak about our lives.

An additional point is that everyone in my family, including my dad and sister, can cook. Because we everybody is handy in the kitchen, none of us needs to wait for one person, such as my mother, to cook for us. Of course, my mother does most of the cooking, but if I come home from school and feel hungry, I can cook food for myself. The ability to cook provides everyone in my family with flexibility that most other families lack.

I enjoy eating meals with everyone in my family, but I do not believe we actually have to do that. We are all busy and know how to cook, so we can eat whenever we have time and are hungry. And we do not chat during meals but speak with one another at other times, so eating together regularly simply is not necessary.

Actual Test 07

TASK 1 Integrated Writing   p. 71

Listening Script

Now listen to part of a lecture on the topic you just read about.

M Professor: Amtrak, the government-owned train service in the United States, is frequently criticized both for the service it provides and for the amount of money it has cost taxpayers in the past few decades. There are constant calls for the government to rid itself of Amtrak by selling it. While I agree with this in principle, I'm not so sure the problems that most people complain about would actually be solved through privatization. Let me tell you why . . .

The most common complaint about Amtrak involves the awful service. I've taken Amtrak before, so I've personally experienced incredibly rude government workers, delays, and even a canceled trip or two. However . . . I've experienced the same problems when I've taken other means of transportation. For instance, how many of you have been subjected to obnoxious

flight attendants on airlines . . . ? Yeah, most of you. I've also experienced numerous delays and canceled flights. And guess what . . . ? None of those airlines was owned by a government. So privatizing Amtrak isn't going to, um, suddenly get rid of those issues.

Now, uh, many people claim that the infrastructure which Amtrak uses is outdated and that the government isn't spending enough money on it. Hmm . . . Well, I have to admit that I agree with those people. However . . . why do people believe the situation will improve if Amtrak is privatized? Fixing Amtrak's infrastructure problems will require billions of dollars. And I seriously doubt a private company will invest that much money into the infrastructure. What's going to happen then? Well, uh, either the government will cover the cost of improving the infrastructure, or the company won't invest enough money to improve everything. So I fail to see the benefit of privatizing Amtrak for safety purposes as well.

Sample Answer

Reading Note

Amtrak should be privatized by government to solve its problems

1 lack of quality service
   – rude employees, slow trains, interrupted service, delays, and cancelations
   – if becomes private company → bad employees can be fired + employees would work better

2 not safe
   – infrastructure is outdated and needs repairing
   – government $ not spent on infrastructure
   – private company → would invest $ to improve infrastructure

Listening Note

Amtrak problems can't be solved through privatization

1 awful service on other means of transportation
   – e.g. bad service on airplanes → aren't government owned
   – privatizing Amtrak won't stop bad service

2 private company won't upgrade infrastructure
   – need billions of $ → company won't invest
   – either government will have to spend money
   – or company won't invest enough → won't improve safety

Sample Essay

During his lecture, the professor discusses what might happen if Amtrak is privatized. While the author of the reading passage contends that most of Amtrak's problems will disappear if it is no longer owned by the government, the professor disagrees with that assertion. He argues that Amtrak's problems will not be solved through privatization.

To start, the professor does not agree with the contention in the reading passage that the horrible service and other problems with Amtrak will go away if the company is privatized. The author of the reading passage claims that a private company will be able to fire people, so the Amtrak employees will improve the quality of their work. But the professor mentions that airlines, which are not government owned, provide terrible service as well. So he does not believe privatizing Amtrak will make the employees work better.

The professor continues by talking about the poor quality of Amtrak's infrastructure. He agrees with the reading passage that the infrastructure is poor. But the author of the reading passage claims that a private company will invest enough money to improve it. The professor, on the other hand, thinks the improvements will cost too much. He says the government will have to pay for the improvements or the company simply will not pay for all of them.

TASK 2 Independent Writing p. 76

Sample Answer 1

Communicate in Person

smaller chance of misunderstanding

– can use lots of time to explain
– email = less info to send / phone = may hear improperly or not understand
– e.g. did group project → spoke face to face → finished early + got highest grade

can brainstorm together

– person gets idea → others get new ideas connected to first one
– team did that while working on project → impossible to do by email or phone

Sample Essay

I can understand why many people would prefer to communicate with their colleagues or classmates by sending email or by talking on the telephone. Nevertheless, I feel that a better way to communicate when working on a project is to speak with people in person.

The primary reason for my feeling this way is that there is a smaller chance of misunderstanding others when you

speak with them in person. When you are standing face to face with someone else, you can use as much time as necessary to explain what needs to be done. If you use email, you are limited in the amount of information you can send. And if you talk over the phone, there is a good chance that others may hear improperly or will not totally understand what you mean. I recently did a group project at my school. There were five team members, including me, and we always met in person to talk about our plans and progress. Since we spoke face to face, we could easily tell if the others understood what we were discussing or knew what to do. We were able to finish our project early, and we got the highest grade in the class. I believe the way we communicated with one another had a lot to do with our grade.

Another benefit to working on projects in person is that people can brainstorm together more easily. When one person gets an idea and says it out loud, others might suddenly come up with new ideas connected to the first one at that same moment. That is exactly what happened to my team on several occasions. One person got a sudden idea, and the others took that idea and immediately came up with ways to improve it by brainstorming. That would have been impossible to do by email or phone.

It is clear to me that communicating in person is better than communicating by email or phone when doing a project involving other people. The group members can avoid misunderstandings, and they can also brainstorm much better by meeting in person. Those two factors will increase the chances of the project being successful.

Sample Answer 2

Communicate through Email or over the Telephone

email

– create written record + useful when others aren't present
– e.g. father couldn't remember work instructions → reread email
– e.g. have idea late at night → send email to others

telephone

– people busy → can't meet in person but have mobile phones
– e.g. want to discuss project → call other group members

Sample Essay

Of the two choices, I prefer the latter. I believe it is better for colleagues and classmates to communicate either by email or phone whenever they are working on a project involving multiple people. Both email and phone communication have their own specific advantages.

One of the main advantages of using email is that it creates a written record of all communication between the people working on a project. This written record can be helpful in a couple of ways. First, if a group member forgets what he or she is supposed to do, the person can always go back, check the email, and confirm what work needs to be done. My father did that on a work project recently. He could not remember everything his team leader had asked him to do. Fortunately, they communicated by email, so he simply reread his email to figure out his assignments. Second, using email communication can be helpful if a person has an idea but the other group members are not present. I often come up with ideas for school projects late at night, but I cannot meet my group members in person then. Instead, I write an email with my thoughts, and I send it to everyone in my group.

As for the telephone, it is also better than meeting face to face. Nowadays, people are very busy and cannot often get together in person. However, almost everyone has access to a telephone, and mobile phones are very common with workers and students alike these days. Thus when a person needs to talk to another group member but that person is not around, the first individual just needs to contact the second one by phone. I do that constantly. When I feel like discussing some aspect of a project with one of my group members, I give that person a call. It does not matter where we are since we can always communicate by using our smartphones.

We live in a modern age when communication devices allow people to talk even if they are not together. I make full use of this by often speaking with my group members by using email or telephones.

TASK 1 Integrated Writing   p. 81

Listening Script

Now listen to part of a lecture on the topic you just read about.

W Professor: Mima mounds, which you can see on the screen here . . . and here . . . are unusual geological formations named after the Mima Prairie in Washington, where they were first closely examined. However, they're found in many arid regions around the world. Despite having been studied extensively, mima mounds are a mystery since geologists aren't exactly sure how they formed. And the three leading theories all have, er, holes in them.

Some geologists claim that the plants growing on mima mounds are responsible for their creation over time. However, look at this picture . . . and this one as well . . . As you can clearly see, not all mima mounds have plants growing on them. And others, like this one . . . only have short grasses on them. I find it highly unlikely that these mounds were created through the actions of plants.

Likewise, I don't believe that mima mounds are created after earthquakes occur. I have a simple explanation for feeling this way. You see, uh, numerous places around the world have mima mounds yet have no history of seismic activity at all. And even in places that have seen a large number of earthquakes in the past few decades, there isn't any evidence of the formation of fresh mima mounds.

Lastly, I also find it doubtful that animals such as gophers have ever made any mima mounds. While gophers do push the soil up when they dig underground, their digging produces nothing nearly as large as mima mounds. It would take several generations of gophers hundreds of years to make just an average-sized mima mound. Oh, and note that some mima mounds, uh, like this one . . . have large stones on top of them. No gopher has the strength to push stones that big high above the ground. It simply can't be done.

Sample Answer

Reading Note

Mima mounds → 3 explanations for formation

1 activity of plants
   – plants grow and roots spread out

– drain area of water and nutrients
– capture soil blown in air and prevent erosion
– build small islands that become mima mounds

2 earthquakes
– tremors cause loose soil to reform in rounded piles
– may be created during earthquakes

3 animals
– gophers build underground dens by pushing up soil
– could make mima mounds over long period of time

Listening Note

Mima mounds formation theories all have problems

1 not all mima mounds have plants
– some have grass / others have nothing
– couldn't have been formed by plants

2 many places w/mima mounds but no earthquakes
– have no seismic activity
– other places w/many earthquakes recently → no fresh mima mounds

3 gophers can't make
– would need several generations of gophers hundreds of years to make small mound
– big rocks on some mima mounds → gophers can't lift

Sample Essay

The professor's lecture is about the formation of mima mounds. She thinks that three of the theories concerning how they are formed have problems, so she casts doubt on the theories that are supported by the author of the reading passage.

The first theory claims that plants are responsible for forming mima mounds. According to the reading passage, plants capture soil and prevent erosion, so, over time, they form mima mounds. The professor disputes this by showing the class some pictures of mima mounds with no plants on them and other mima mounds that have only grass on them. She says that no plants formed those mima mounds.

The second theory credits earthquakes with creating mima mounds. The author of the reading passage writes that earthquakes can cause loose soil to be arranged into piles. However, the professor points out that there are many places which get no earthquakes yet have mima mounds. She also notes that other places which have had many earthquakes recently do not have any new mima mounds.

The third theory is that gophers, which dig underground passages, form mima mounds. The professor declares that it would take a large number of gophers centuries to make a small mima mound. Thus she believes it would be impossible for gophers to make them.

TASK 2 Independent Writing p. 86

Sample Answer 1

Agree

neat clothes = neat, well-organized personality
– aunt → neat clothes = organized and clean
– friend → sloppy clothes = room is messy

flashy clothes = negative personality
– self-centered or think are better than others
– girls at school → bright & expensive clothes = terrible personalities

Sample Essay

It is true that the way a person dresses is a good indication of that individual's personality and character. I have frequently noticed this about a large number of people, which is why I agree with the statement.

One thing I have noticed is that how neatly a person dresses is almost always an indicator of how neat or organized that person actually is. As a general rule, if a person makes sure his or her clothes are neat and look presentable at all times, then that individual has a neat and well-organized personality. For example, my aunt wears very neat clothes. They are never wrinkled, and all of her clothing always matches. She is also extremely well organized and clean. Her home is never messy or disorganized but instead looks very nice. On the other hand, one of my friends frequently wears sloppy clothes. It should come as no surprise that his bedroom is very messy and has clothes, books, and even empty food wrappers lying all over the floor.

Another thing I have noticed is that people who wear clothes which are very flashy tend to have negative personality characteristics. Many of these people are self-centered, or they think of themselves as better than others. Several girls at my school like to wear brightly colored clothes and accessories that are clearly expensive. They have some of the worst personalities of all the people I have ever met. They are not only mean to other students, but they are also extremely conceited. Basically, they act as if the world revolves around them. I have seen many other people with negative personalities. In nearly every instance, I could tell by the clothes they were wearing that they had unappealing characteristics.

I think you can tell a lot about a person by observing the clothes that he or she is wearing. You can typically determine if the person has either negative or positive characteristics.

Disagree

messy clothes ≠ messy life
- teacher → wrinkled clothes
- has neat classroom / lectures are well organized

expensive clothes ≠ egotistical person
- father = VP at corp. → expensive clothes
- people think is snob or has neg. personality
- but is down-to-earth person

Sample Essay

I do not think it is possible to determine a person's personality and characteristics just by looking at the clothes that he or she is wearing. As a result, I disagree with the statement.

Many people believe that a person who wears messy clothes may be messy in general while a person who wears neat and clean clothes is both neat and clean in other aspects of life. But my observations have shown me that this is not true on numerous occasions. One of my teachers at school always wears shirts and pants that are wrinkled. I do not think he has ever ironed any of his clothes even once. You might think he would be a messy person, but that is far from the case. His classroom is extremely neat, and his lectures are always well organized. The only part about him that is messy is his clothes.

In addition, there are many people who wear expensive and flashy clothes which are designed to attract people's attention, but they are not egotistical and do not believe themselves better than others. My father is a great example of this kind of person. He is a vice president at a major corporation, so he has to wear expensive suits to work every day. You can tell merely by looking at his suits that they cost a great deal of money. Many people therefore believe my father is a snob or has a negative personality. But he is actually one of the most down-to-earth people I know. People regularly comment on how kind and considerate he is, and they never say anything negative about his personality.

People like my teacher at school and my father are proof that you cannot judge a person's personality according to the clothes he or she wears. If someone looked at

them—or many other people—and tried to figure out what kind of person each is, then that individual would definitely be incorrect.

Actual Test 09

TASK 1 Integrated Writing
p. 91

Now listen to part of a lecture on the topic you just read about.

M Professor: As we just learned, the Dust Bowl caused various problems on the Great Plains throughout the 1930s. The period was characterized by wind that picked up loose topsoil and blew it across the prairie in the guise of enormous dust storms. In recent years, while many people have started blaming the farmers for what happened, they are quite mistaken in their accusations.

First of all, American farmers had been raising crops on the Great Plains ever since the nineteenth century. Year after year, they planted their crops, and the prairieland yielded abundant harvests. Then, in the 1920s, due to various events happening around the world, the global demand for wheat increased. American farmers did what any rational person would do: They broke more land to grow more wheat. And remember that when the Great Depression started in 1929, the prices of crops crashed. So many farmers, again, uh, quite rationally, responded by planting more crops. They were simply trying to get back some of the money they had lost. So it's, um, it's unfair to blame the rapid increase in the amount of land being farmed on the farmers.

Additionally, remember that there had been no severe droughts on the Great Plains for more than three decades. Most of those farmers hadn't been living there in the 1890s since they were new immigrants, so they had no personal experience with that drought. And methods commonly used to prevent soil erosion today were little known in the 1930s. Others were quite unfeasible. For instance, yes, growing trees would have helped prevent wind erosion, but trees take years to grow. And leaving fields fallow to let prairie grass grow would have cut into farmers' already-slim profit margins. And that's why it's not right to blame the Dust Bowl on the farmers.

Reading Note

1930s Dust Bowl → made worse by farmers

1 lots of land on Great Plains used for farming
   – Russia no longer sells foodstuffs abroad
     → American farmers plant more wheat
   – 5 million new acres on Great Plains → used for farming
   – soil conditions bad → needed moisture
   – less rain in 1930s → land became barren

2 farmers didn't act to stop erosion
   – bad drought in 1890s → farmers should have remembered
   – didn't protect topsoil from erosion
   – didn't plant trees or let land remain fallow
   – actions let wind blow away topsoil → caused dust storms

Listening Note

Shouldn't blame farmers for Dust Bowl

1 was natural to break more land
   – demand for wheat went up → farmers broke more land
   – Great Depression in 1929 → prices of crops went down
   – farmers planted more crops → wanted to get back $ they lost

2 farmers didn't know how to protect land
   – most Great Plains farmers = new immigrants
     → didn't know about 1890s drought
   – modern soil erosion methods unknown then
   – growing trees → takes years
   – leaving land fallow → cut into farmers' profit margins

Sample Essay

The professor lectures about the Dust Bowl, which happened in the 1930s in the Great Plains in the United States. The professor believes that American farmers were not responsible for what happened. In his lecture, he challenges the arguments made in the reading passage, which blames American farmers for making the Dust Bowl worse.

The professor starts by saying that American farmers planted crops in the Great Plains for many years and were rewarded with abundant harvests. According to him, when the global demand for wheat rose, the farmers naturally planted more wheat, especially since the Great Depression was causing them financial hardship. In those two ways, he counters the argument made in the

reading passage that the farmers should have known the land in the Great Plains was unsuitable for farming.

Next, the professor points out that many farmers in the Great Plains were recent immigrants to the country so were unaware of the drought in the 1890s. This contrasts the claim in the reading passage that many farmers knew what had happened in the drought. The reading passage also declares that the farmers could have acted to lessen the effects of erosion on the soil. However, the professor mentions that many methods of preventing erosion were unknown in the 1930s or were impractical because they would have taken years to implement.

TASK 2 Independent Writing   p. 96

Agree

had same problem in past
– can give good advice
– had problem w/teacher → talked to older friend
– had same issue → explained her solution → worked

have more experience
– may know someone who had same problem
– bro → 5 years older = more life experience
– gives relevant advice from friends' lives

have different perspectives
– wanted to go to b'day party → parents said no
– older friend said to look from parents' point of view
   → stopped being mad

Sample Essay

I find myself in agreement with the statement. It is obviously better to get advice from my older friends than from my friends who are the same age as me.

To begin with, my older friends are likely to have dealt with the same problem in the past. They will therefore be able to provide me with advice on what I should and should not to do solve my problem. Two weeks ago, I had a problem with one of my teachers. I spoke with a friend who is two years older than me. She mentioned that she had had the same issue with that teacher in the past. Then, she told me how she had fixed the problem. I tried her solution, and it worked perfectly.

Another thing is that older friends have more experience, so while they might not have had the same issues themselves, they might know someone who has. My brother is five years older than me, so he has much more life experience. Nearly every time I need advice, I tell him what is going on in my life. There have been numerous instances when he has told me, "This never happened to me, but it happened to a friend of mine." Then, he provides relevant advice that is based on the experiences of his friends.

A third point that causes me to agree with the statement is that older people have different perspectives. This makes them look at problems in ways that do not often occur to me. The other day, I was upset with my parents because I wanted to go to my friend's birthday party, but they insisted that I stay home to complete a school project I was working on. I was really angry until a friend older than me gave me some advice. He said I needed to consider my parents' point of view. While I was thinking of immediate fun, they were thinking about my future and the importance of doing well in school. Because of his advice, I stopped being mad at my parents.

I always go to my older friends when I need advice. They have dealt with the same problems before, they have more experience so know people who have had the same problems, and they look at situations differently. Those three reasons result in them providing me with excellent advice.

Sample Answer 2

Disagree

are closest friends

– know me better than anyone else → can give advice
– had recent problem → best advice was from friend the same age

older friends = can't see relevance of problems

– say, "Don't worry about it; no big deal"
  → but is important to me
– friends same age see relevance → try to help

have same experiences

– same grade, same experiences, & know same people
– understand my problems best → can provide best advice

Sample Essay

While I can understand why some people would agree with the statement, I personally disagree with it. I have a number of personal experiences which make me believe that this statement is incorrect.

First, my friends who are the same age as me are my closest friends. These people know me much better than anyone else—even my family members—does. That fact makes them the best people to give me advice. When I had a recent personal problem, several people, including family members, teachers, and older friends, gave me some advice. However, by far the best advice I received

came from a friend my age. She told me to do something that nobody else had suggested. I followed her advice, and my situation improved a great deal.

Second, my friends who are older than me often have difficulty understanding me because of the age difference. Basically, they fail to see the relevance of my problems. If I mention something that is bothering me to them, they might respond, "Oh, it's no big deal. Don't worry about it." To them, the problem is not relevant, so they regard it as something minor. However, it is of great importance to me, and my friends who are the same age as me usually recognize that, so they try to help.

Third, my friends who are the same age as me have the same experiences that I do. They are in the same grade at school, they experience the same problems, and they know most of the same people. Those three features make them singularly suited for understanding my problems and how they can be solved in the best manner. There have been several instances in the past year when I have needed advice for personal and school problems, and friends the same age as me helped me out the best each time.

Friends older than me can provide good advice, but the best advice always comes from my friends who are the same age as me. They know me the best, and they understand my problems perfectly, so that enables them to advise me better than anyone else can.

Actual Test 10

TASK 1 Integrated Writing   p. 101

Listening Script

Now listen to part of a lecture on the topic you just read about.

W Professor: Paleontologists have an ongoing debate concerning whether early mammals were dinosaur hunters or merely scavenged their carcasses. Much of this debate centers on the fossil of a single species, so the evidence is quite slim. The fossil is of a small mammal called *R. robustus*, which contained the fossilized body of a baby dinosaur, uh, a psittacosaur, inside it. Here's a picture of it . . . The controversy regarding it concerns whether *R. robustus* hunted and killed the dinosaur or simply devoured its body.

Most of my colleagues believe *R. robustus* was a scavenger, but I disagree and believe it was a hunter. We must remember that when *R. robustus* lived, there were numerous species of small dinosaurs. It's entirely possible that *R. robustus* specialized in hunting small dinosaurs or baby dinosaurs of larger species. It surely left full-grown adults alone.

Don't be dissuaded by the odd body shape of *R. robustus* either. Yes, it had short legs and a squat body. But do you know what . . . ? So does the Tasmanian devil, and it excels as a hunter. In addition, if *R. robustus* specialized in hunting baby dinosaurs, as I believe it did, then it surely didn't require blinding speed to catch and kill them.

Many paleontologists proclaim that the lack of bite marks on the bones of the baby psittacosaur fossil proves *R. robustus* didn't hunt and kill it. But, well, it's entirely possible that *R. robustus* didn't bite all the way to the animal's bones. Perhaps it only bit the animal in its flesh. Or it may have killed the baby dinosaur with its claws and then swallowed it by gulping, not chewing. We simply can't claim that *R. robustus* was a scavenger based on the evidence—or lack of evidence—from a single fossil.

Sample Answer

Reading Note

Mammal *R. robustus* was scavenger of dinosaurs

1 **small size**
   - smaller than most dinosaurs → probably didn't attack them
   - body of psittacosaur in fossil = baby → smaller than adult

2 **body shape**
   - short legs + squat body → no speed
   - ran w/awkward gait
   - couldn't chase down and kill dinosaurs

3 **no teeth marks on bones**
   - didn't attack, kill, and chew on dinosaurs
   - came across it after it had died

Listening Note

R. robustus was hunter

1 **were many small dinosaurs**
   - could have specialized in hunting them
   - could have hunted babies, too

2 **body shape wasn't problem**
   - Tasmanian devil = excellent hunter

   - hunted baby dinosaurs → didn't need great speed

3 **might not have bitten to bones**
   - could have bitten the animal's flesh
   - or killed the baby w/claws
   - can't claim it was a scavenger from one fossil

Sample Essay

The professor's lecture covers the debate regarding the mammal *R. robustus*. While the author of the reading passage believes *R. robustus* was a scavenger, the professor casts doubt on this notion and claims it hunted small dinosaurs.

The professor points out that there many small dinosaurs living at the same time as *R. robustus*. She thinks *R. robustus* hunted and ate those dinosaurs as well as baby dinosaurs of other species. Thus she casts doubt on the argument in the reading passage that *R. robustus* was too small to hunt dinosaurs.

The next point concerns the body of *R. robustus*. The reading passage mentions that its body shape made it a poor hunter. But the professor mentions that the body shape of *R. robustus* was similar to that of the Tasmanian devil, and she says it is an excellent hunter. She further notes that *R. robustus* may have hunted babies, so it did not need speed to hunt well.

Last of all, the professor covers the lack of bite marks on the bones of the baby dinosaur in the fossilized body of *R. robustus*. According to the reading passage, the absence of bite marks proves that *R. robustus* scavenged the body. Yet the professor claims that *R. robustus* might not have bitten through to the bone or could have killed the dinosaur with its claws.

TASK 2 Independent Writing p. 106

Sample Answer 1

Agree

can become more creative
- math, language, science, and history → don't use imagination
- study art and music → can be more creative
- e.g. drew a lot when young → have creative mind

need to make school interesting
- art and music = fun classes
- e.g. nephew loves music class → favorite subject

discover child prodigies
- young people can excel at art and music
- need to take classes to expose their talents
- can find geniuses like Mozart

I fully agree with the statement. In my opinion, all children between the ages of five and ten should have to study both art and music in addition to other standard subjects at school. I have three reasons for feeling this way.

The first is that the study of art and music can help young people become more creative. When children only study subjects such as math, language, science, and history, they almost never exercise their imaginations. Instead, they simply learn facts and memorize data. On the other hand, when children study art and music, they use their imaginations and become more creative. I have a very creative mind, and I think much of that has to do with the fact that I drew constantly when I was young. If more children could study art and music, they might develop creative minds as well.

Another reason is that children need to partake in fun activities to make school more interesting for them. While math, language, and other subjects are important, they are not particularly exciting. Many children need a reason to look forward to going to school, and having art and music classes can provide this reason. My nephew is seven, and he is always talking about how much fun he has in his music class in school. It is easily his favorite subject.

A third reason is that by providing art and music classes, schools can help discover child prodigies in those two fields. Art and music are two subjects that young people can excel at. However, if they are not exposed to these subjects, their talents might never be discovered. We need to remember that geniuses such as Mozart were composing music when they were very young. By having art and music classes, schools might help us find more young people like Mozart, which would benefit society in general.

Schools should definitely require their young students to study art and music in addition to other subjects. The students will become more creative and have fun, and it will be possible to find child prodigies. Those reasons make me agree with the statement.

Sample Answer 2

Disagree

many students hate art and music
- shouldn't force them to take classes they hate
- can't draw → teachers and students make fun of my pictures
- am tone deaf → can't sing + feel bad in class

too many subjects at school
- already have enough classes
- if add two more classes, then school day becomes longer
- or shorten more important classes

have to hire more teachers
- economy isn't good
- schools' funding decreased
- can't afford to hire new teachers

On the surface, the proposal in the statement does not seem too bad. Nevertheless, I am opposed to it. I do not think students should be forced to study art and music in addition to their other subjects.

One reason is that many students absolutely hate art and music, so schools should not force them to study subjects that they strongly dislike. I have no artistic ability at all. As a result, I have always despised going to art class. I am not good at drawing, and the teachers and other students sometimes make fun of my pictures. I am also tone deaf and cannot sing well, so I feel bad in music class, too. Large numbers of students are like me. We cannot stand those two subjects and should not be forced to take them.

Another problem is that young students already study enough subjects at school, so they should not be forced to learn even more of them. Most elementary school students study math, history, social studies, language, and science, and they also have gym class. That is enough classes for young students. If two more classes are added, then either the school day will become longer, or more important classes will be shortened. Neither of those two should happen.

Last of all, requiring students to study art and music means that most schools will have to hire several new teachers. These days, the economy in my country is not particularly good, and many school districts are seeing their funding reduced, especially for the study of foreign languages. These school districts cannot afford to hire new art and music teachers, particularly when they are getting rid of some of their foreign language teachers. So schools should not require students to take classes when they cannot afford to pay the teachers for those classes.

Students like myself dislike art and music and should not be obligated to study them. Likewise, students already study too many subjects, and many school districts have no money to hire new art and music teachers. For those three reasons, I disagree with the statement.

Actual Test 11

TASK 1 Integrated Writing
p. 111

Listening Script

Now listen to part of a lecture on the topic you just read about.

M Professor: Take a look at this . . . and this . . . and this . . . These are images of some ancient structures in the Andes Mountains in Peru. Archaeologists have long believed that these places didn't have a military purpose but instead served other functions. A recently published book makes some compelling arguments that these structures were indeed military forts though.

Now, uh, you may notice the lack of an outer wall surrounding this structure . . . and this one . . . Normally, the absence of a wall would automatically disqualify a building as a defensive structure. However . . . the book points out that many Peruvian forts relied upon natural defenses, such as steep cliffs, to serve as barriers to prevent attackers from gaining entrance. Thus the builders didn't waste time making walls when they weren't needed.

The book's author further claims that the lack of parapets on the walls and the fact that the walls had many outer doors wasn't uncommon. He states that primitive societies around the world constructed forts with simple walls and no parapets. Likewise, the numerous doors were necessary because they enabled the defenders to leave the forts in great numbers to drive off any foes that approached too close to them.

The author points out that the great distance of the forts from their neighboring villages wasn't a problem since the villagers usually had ample warning of any impending attacks. Therefore, uh, they had plenty of time to reach the forts. The author further discounts the absence of wells in the forts. He states that sieges in the Andes Mountains were uncommon. After all, the attackers would have had to bring large amounts of food and water to lay siege to a fort. In a mountainous region like the Andes, that was too difficult a task for most armies, so they almost never tried.

Sample Answer

Reading Note

Andes Mountain forts in Peru → were probably not defensive bases

1 **didn't have defense measures**
  – many lacked walls surrounding interior buildings
  – would have let attackers overtake them easily

2 **had poor defenses**
  – walls lacked parapets
  – walls had many doorways → easy access points for attackers

3 **were in poor locations**
  – far from villages → couldn't have been refuges
  – no internal water sources → would have been doomed if besieged

Listening Note

Structures were military forts

1 **didn't need walls**
  – used natural defenses like steep cliffs
  – served as barriers against attackers

2 **no parapets + many doors = common**
  – primitive societies made simple walls w/no parapets
  – doors let many defenders leave forts to attack

3 **location of forts wasn't problem**
  – villagers had ample warning before attack
    → could get to forts in plenty of time
  – were rarely sieges in Andes Mountains
  – attackers needed their own food and water
    → difficult to carry w/them

Sample Essay

The professor's lecture focuses on the purpose of some ancient forts in the Andes Mountains in Peru. According to the reading passage, it is unlikely that they had a military purpose. However, the professor's lecture answers the questions raised in the reading passage and explains why these places probably were military forts.

The professor begins by focusing on the lack of outer walls at some forts. In the reading passage, the absence of walls proves that the forts were not military bases because attackers could have easily gained entrance to them. The professor, however, comments that the builders used natural defenses, such as cliffs, in place of walls, so walls were occasionally unnecessary.

Next, the professor discusses the lack of parapets and the presence of numerous doors in the walls. While these are regarded as weaknesses in the reading passage, the professor notes that many primitive cultures built simple walls with no parapets. Additionally, the doors enabled multiple defenders to emerge simultaneously to combat the enemy.

Finally, the professor discusses the locations of the

forts and the absence of wells in them. He claims that villagers would have known about approaching enemies, so they surely had enough time to reach the forts. And since laying siege to mountain forts was difficult, the lack of a water supply was not an issue for the defenders.

TASK 2 Independent Writing p. 116

Sample Answer 1

Information from the Media

media organization = websites, magazines, etc.

– discuss advantages and disadvantages of items
– e.g. parents wanted a computer → got info from media group website → made good purchase

TV news reports

– focus on faults of products
– e.g. uncle wanted to buy car → saw news report → bought safer one

blogs

– entries and comments helpful
– e.g. learned about computer game → enjoy it a lot

Sample Essay

Some people like getting advice from their friends, salespeople, and themselves prior to making important purchases. I am not one of those people though. As for me, I almost always get information from the media and make my decisions based on what I learn from a variety of sources.

First of all, there are many media organizations dedicated to discussing the advantages and disadvantages of various items, including automobiles and electronic products. These organizations typically have websites, magazines, or other ways to publicize their analyses of products. Recently, my parents were considering buying a computer, so they visited the website of a media group and learned about the different types of computers available for purchase. They were able to use that information to purchase an inexpensive yet efficient computer that everyone in my family currently uses.

It is also possible to watch TV news reports about some products. As a general rule, news reports on products focus upon their faults. However, the faults they mention are commonly ones that could harm or kill users. For instance, my uncle was considering buying a car recently. He had decided on a specific make and model, but then he happened to watch the news one night. It featured a report on that exact car and how its airbags had serious problems. Thanks to the media, my uncle did not buy that car but instead bought a safer one.

Finally, I find blogs to be extremely helpful when I am trying to decide what to buy. I visit several blogs that focus on consumer products. The entries by the blog owners are helpful, and so are the comments the readers leave. A while ago, I bought a new computer game thanks to a blog entry and the comments made about it. I love the game and play it constantly, but I would not have known about it if I had not read that particular blog.

In my opinion, getting information from the media is the best way to make a decision when buying something big. There are media organizations that describe the benefits and drawbacks of products, news shows can focus on dangerous products, and blog entries and comments can also provide more information. Altogether, they make the media my primary source for information on items I am considering buying.

Sample Answer 2

Their Own Opinions

people know what they like and want

– other people → cannot look into person's mind
– e.g. father got recommended car → wasn't one he wanted

trust research on items they buy

– e.g. sis researched smartphones
– salesman recommended phone → sis bought phone she wanted → is happy

know how much $ can spend

– e.g. parents wanted new apartment
– friends and agents recommended → parents got house could afford → like house

Sample Essay

When people are considering buying something important, they often get advice or information from a wide variety of sources. However, I believe that they should listen the most to themselves and that they should make their own advice be the deciding factor in determining what to purchase.

The main reason I suggest this is that people know best what they like and want. While other people can provide advice, they cannot look into a person's mind and see what that individual really thinks about something. My father was shopping for a car recently. He listened to several different people and read many online reviews of automobiles. He got the car which was the most recommended, but it was not the car he wanted. Because of that, he is incredibly unhappy and hates driving the car.

Another is that people ought to trust their own research about the items that they buy. Two months ago, my older sister was planning to buy a smartphone. She did a lot of research on the different models that were available. When she went to the store, the salesman tried to get her to buy the newest and most expensive model. However, she knew from her research that she did not want that model, so she got the one that her research had indicated would be the best smartphone for her. By trusting herself, my sister made a good decision on her purchase.

A third reason for people to listen to themselves is that they know how much money they can afford to spend. When my parents were shopping for a new apartment, they had a firm budget which they refused to depart from. They looked at some places they liked and which their friends and real estate agents had recommended, but those apartments were too expensive for them. Instead, they trusted their own opinion and got a house they could afford and which all of us like.

There are many ways to get advice when buying something important, but it is always better for people to trust themselves. They know best what they want, they know what their research tells them, and they know how much they can afford to pay. By trusting themselves, people can make the best possible purchase.

Actual Test 12

TASK 1 Integrated Writing

p. 121

Listening Script

Now listen to part of a lecture on the topic you just read about.

W Professor: While many people nowadays declare that homeschooling is the best way to solve the country's education problems, I wholeheartedly disagree. I think parents who homeschool their children are doing them a great disservice. Instead, parents ought to enroll their children in the nation's public schools, where they can be taught alongside most of the country's other children.

Now, uh, most supporters of homeschooling frequently brag about the numerous surveys showing that homeschooled children get better grades and are more accomplished than their public school counterparts.

Well, uh, to be blunt, those statistics are skewed. You see, uh, there are only about two million homeschooled students in the country. You can't compare them with the tens of millions of students who attend public schools. I mean, uh, it's impossible to compare such a small sample with a much larger one.

Now, um, many parents claim they homeschool their children to spend more time with them. That's admirable, but most of these parents are completely unqualified to teach their children. Remember that most parents aren't credentialed teachers, so they not only don't know the subjects they're teaching their children, but they also don't know the most recent teaching methods. Therefore, these parents are putting their children at a disadvantage by trying to educate them.

Finally, homeschooled children aren't being socialized the way children at public schools are. Thus children being taught at their homes won't develop the same social skills that others will, so they might not fit in well with others. Homeschoolers will also miss out on important activities, such as school dances, clubs, and the opportunities to play sports, and they'll likely have fewer friends by not attending school. It seems clear to me, uh, that parents shouldn't homeschool their children but should instead send them to public schools.

Sample Answer

Reading Note

Homeschooling = better than learning at public schools

1 get better educations
  - statistics show perform better than public school students
  - more complete high school and go to university
  - outperform public school students at university

2 social advantages
  - brings parents and children closer together
  - no bullying
  - no violent students and unmotivated teachers

3 rarely have behavioral issues
  - better at social interactions
  - take part in after-school activities → interact with both children and adults

Listening Note

Parents shouldn't homeschool their children

1 performance statistics are skewed
  - 2 million homeschoolers vs. 10s of millions of public school students

– can't compare small sample with large sample

2 **parents are unqualified**
   – not credentialed teachers
   – don't know subjects or teaching methods

3 **aren't socialized like public school children**
   – won't develop social skills → might not fit in well w/ others
   – miss out on social activities → may have fewer friends

Sample Essay

In her lecture, the professor speaks as an opponent of homeschooling and comes out in favor of children attending public schools. The points she raises in her lecture challenge some of the specific claims that are made in the reading passage.

First, the professor refutes the contention in the reading passage that homeschooled children do better than children at public schools. She points out that there are only two million homeschooled children but tens of millions of students at public schools. She argues that it is impossible to compare the performances of the two.

Then, the professor declares that homeschooled children are being put at a disadvantage by their parents since they are not credentialed teachers. According to her, their parents do not know the subjects they are teaching or any current teaching methods. Her arguments go against the claim in the reading passage that homeschooled children benefit by avoiding bullying, violence, and teachers who do not care.

Lastly, the professor says that homeschooled children do not get socialized like children at public schools do. As a result, they will not develop social skills and will have fewer friends. This argument goes against the one in the reading passage, which claims that homeschooled children have few behavioral issues and are able to speak well with both children and adults.

TASK 2 Independent Writing

p. 126

Sample Answer 1

Agree

helps them get into good universities and get good jobs
   – m.s. grades are important → must care about them
   – h.s. students must do well at school + do extracurricular activities → must plan ahead for future
   – e.g. sis did well at school + joined right clubs → went to elite college → got outstanding job

modern life = complex
   – many things for young people to do
   – e.g. attend school / take extra classes / play soccer / volunteer / do homework → must be well-organized

Sample Essay

Modern life is much more complex than it was a few decades ago. Therefore, it is essential for young people to have the ability to plan and organize if they want to be successful.

Many people define success as getting into a good university, graduating, and then finding a job which they like and pays a good salary. To accomplish these goals, young people must be able to plan well. Nowadays, even students' grades in middle school are important, so young people need to care about their academic abilities when they are in their early teens. High school students not only have to do well at school but also have to participate in extracurricular activities. Which ones they do typically depends on what they want to study during their university years, so they need to think ahead and make plans for the future. My older sister did this very well. She started planning her life when she was in middle school. She excelled at school and joined the right clubs, so she got accepted to an elite university. After graduating, she landed an outstanding job at an architectural firm, where she is presently employed.

Young people additionally must be able to organize well due to the complexity of modern life. There are so many things young people need to do nowadays. I am a perfect example of this. I attend school five days a week and take extra classes after school. I study math at an academy, and a private tutor visits my house to teach me the violin. Furthermore, I play on a soccer team and do five hours of volunteer work weekly. And, of course, I have to do my homework once I arrive home every night. I have to be extremely well-organized to remember to do everything and to do these activities well. If I forget even one thing, I can cause problems for myself for a long time.

Young people definitely must be able to plan and organize well if they want to be successful in life. Modern life is too complex, so without those two skills, youths will most likely end up failing at whatever they are doing.

Sample Answer 2

Disagree

some people = spontaneous
   – make decisions or act instantly
   – e.g. cousin never plans → got good job + makes lots

of money

some people = lucky

- lives work out thanks to good luck
- e.g. friend's sis = disorganized + doesn't care about future → went to good school + got good job

Sample Essay

Being able to plan and being organized are two skills most people would love to have. Yet no matter how complex modern life is, I do not believe a person must possess those abilities to be successful, so I disagree with the statement.

There are some people who have no need to plan ahead because they excel at being spontaneous. They can make decisions or act instantly, and whatever they do seems to succeed most of the time. My cousin is one of these people. He is in his mid-twenties, and I do not believe he has ever planned anything in his life. It seems like he just makes up his mind to do something and then does it. He did not attend a great university, but that has not prevented him from being successful. He has an excellent job and earns a lot of money, yet it is in a field that he never expressed any interest in during his youth. He simply decided to apply for the job one day and got hired. I do not know how he manages to be successful, but his spontaneity has benefitted him a great deal.

There are also people who are lucky. They might not be well-organized, and they might lack the ability to plan ahead, but their lives still work out well mostly because of what people call good luck. My best friend's sister is the luckiest person I know. She is ten years older than me. She is incredibly disorganized, and she never thinks about the future, but everything always works out well for her. She never cared about middle school or high school, but she got good grades. She was accepted to a good school despite the fact that she had no interest in where she went. And after she graduated, she got offered a job in another city after she applied for the job when she saw an advertisement on a random website on the Internet. In her case, she has gotten by thanks to luck rather than through planning or organizing.

Most people would love to be good planners and organizers, but they do not have to be either to succeed in modern society. Both my cousin and my friend's sister are proof of that.

Actual Test 13

TASK 1 Integrated Writing

p. 131

Listening Script

Now listen to part of a lecture on the topic you just read about.

M Professor: Just last week in New Zealand, a large pod of whales stranded themselves on a beach. Sadly, dozens of them died before people could help the rest get back to deeper water. Why whales, uh, and dolphins, too, beach themselves isn't fully understood. There are two main theories which most members of the marine biology community believe account for their actions, but I believe each of them has some problems. Let me tell you why . . .

Many marine biologists claim that whales and dolphins get beached when they swim close to shore to feed on fish. Others claim that the leader of a pod may become sick, and the rest of the pod refuses to abandon it after it swims into shallow water. Well, uh, those sound interesting, but they both have problems. First of all, examinations of the whales and dolphins that die after beaching themselves show that most have empty stomachs, so they couldn't have been feeding. Likewise, autopsies of beached whales and dolphins have shown that none—I repeat, none—of them was suffering any diseases at all.

What about the other main theory? Well, there actually is a great deal of evidence that naval sonar waves can harm the brains of whales and dolphins and that this could account for some mammals beaching themselves. However, this doesn't happen every time the world's navies use their sonar. In fact, it's an extremely rare occurrence. And keep in mind that many beached whales and dolphins show no signs of brain damage and that they often beach themselves very far away from where any naval activity has taken place. So it seems to me that there must be some other reasons that these animals are beaching themselves.

Sample Answer

Reading Note

2 theories on why whales and dolphins beach themselves

1 head into shallow water and get trapped there
   - follow schools of fish to feed

- follow sick leader going to shallow water to die
- get trapped when tides goes out
- too tired when tide comes back in to swim to deep water

2 damaged by sonar of naval ships
- brains damaged by sonar systems
- happened in Bahamas in 2000
- four incidents of whales beaching themselves
- had suffered damage to brains and internal organs

Listening Note

Both leading theories have problems

1 don't head to shallow water to feed or to follow leader
- most have empty stomachs → weren't feeding
- autopsies show none had diseases → weren't sick

2 sonar isn't a problem in all beaching incidents
- is rare occurrence
- many whales and dolphins have no brain damage
- beach themselves far from naval activity

Sample Essay

During his lecture, the professor talks about the reasons that whales and dolphins beach themselves. He mentions two theories which many people think are correct, but he states that he disagrees with both of them. His arguments cast doubt on the points made in the reading passage.

The professor notes that many marine biologists believe whales and dolphins get trapped in shallow water when they are feeding on fish or when they follow a sick pod member swimming toward shore. According to the reading passage, these animals get trapped in shallow water and are then washed ashore. However, the professor believes they are not feeding since the animals rarely have food in their stomachs. He also says that the whales and dolphins show no signs of disease, so they are not sick either.

Another popular theory is that the sonar systems of naval ships are causing brain damage in whales and dolphins. According to the reading passage, the resulting brain damage makes the mammals beach themselves. The professor agrees that many whales and dolphins are injured by the sonar, but he claims that this happens rarely. He also points out that the animals often beach themselves far away from places where naval ships were. So he does not consider human naval activity a primary reason the animals are beaching themselves.

TASK 2 Independent Writing p. 136

Sample Answer 1

Agree

earn money
- don't have to get $ from parents
- e.g. both sisters worked → had own spending $

gain work experience
- helpful for future
- e.g. one sis learned very much from p-t job
- learned to deal w/customers, do office work, and follow schedule

help decide on college major
- e.g. other sis didn't know what to study
- worked at vet's office one summer → liked job → studying to be vet now

Sample Essay

I believe that people should start working part time at a young age for a number of different reasons. Therefore, I fully agree with the statement that high school students should be encouraged by their parents to find part-time jobs during their summer vacations.

The first reason I support this is the most obvious one: to earn money. Many high school students rely upon their parents for their spending money, but if they were to get part-time jobs during their summer breaks, then they would not have to ask their mother and father for any money. Both of my older sisters worked part time when they were in high school. As a result, they had their own spending money and never had to ask my parents for an allowance.

A second advantage of working part time is that high school students can gain valuable work experience. Even if they are planning to attend college and will not seek employment immediately after graduating from high school, this experience can be extremely valuable for the future. One of my sisters constantly mentions that she learned a great deal from her summer part-time job. She learned how to deal with customers, how to do office work, and how to follow a schedule. For her, the part-time job she had was very important.

A final benefit of working part time during summer is that it can help young people decide on a major when they attend college. For the longest time, my other sister was not sure what she wanted to study at college. Then, one summer, she worked part time at a veterinarian's office. She discovered she loved working with animals and was good at it, so she majored in biology and is currently studying to be a veterinarian. In her case, working part time helped determine the course of her entire life.

Clearly, working part time during summer has many advantages for high school students. They can earn money, get experience, and decide on their future majors. It is obvious to me that parents should encourage their high school-aged children to work part time during their summer vacations.

Sample Answer 2

Disagree

do other activities

– take summer classes, travel abroad, or do volunteer work
– no time to work

need to rest

– h.s. students constantly busy → exhausted
– e.g. older bro → rested at home after long semester → has a great job

don't need money

– wealthy families → give $ to children
– e.g. friend's bro = rich → gets $ from parents when needs

Sample Essay

I think there are many high school students who would benefit greatly from working part time during their summer vacations. However, I disagree with the statement because I do not believe that parents should encourage their children in high school to find part-time jobs.

For one thing, there are many high school students who engage in activities which prevent them from working part time during their summer vacations. For instance, a lot of high school students take classes during summer vacation in order to improve their knowledge in various subjects. Others travel abroad with their families. And there are some high school students who volunteer at charities, churches, or other places. None of these individuals has time to work during summer vacation, even on a part-time basis.

For another thing, the high school students in my country are constantly busy during the semester. They start school early in the morning and finish late at night. Many of them additionally have private tutors or go to academies after school is finished. When summer vacation comes, the best thing for them to do is to take a break. My older brother used to spend most of his summer vacation resting at home because he was simply exhausted after the grueling spring semester. He

currently has a great job, so not working during summer did not affect him negatively.

Last of all, the main reason anyone gets a job is to make money, but there are many high school students who have no need to earn money. In most of these cases, they come from wealthy families, so their parents are able to give them money when they need it. The brother of one of my friends is in high school. His family is rich, so he never works during summer vacation. His parents simply give him money whenever he asks for some, and he does other activities during the break.

It is not ideal for parents to encourage their children attending high school to find part-time jobs during their summer vacations. Many do other activities in summer, others rest because of their busy semesters, and others have no need to earn money by working part time.

Actual Test 14

TASK 1 Integrated Writing

p. 141

Listening Script

Now listen to part of a lecture on the topic you just read about.

W Professor: In the United States, the government subsidizes farmers by paying them approximately forty-four billion dollars annually. While some people claim that subsidies have advantages, I intensely dislike them and believe they should be abolished.

My primary problem with subsidies is that I don't believe farmers should be paid not to work or if they fail to produce any food to sell. Yes, uh, being a farmer is risky, but so is, um, pretty much every business venture. I'm a firm believer in the free market and don't think people should be guaranteed cash not to work or if they have problems. Furthermore, I couldn't care less about using subsidies to entice the children of farmers to remain on farms. Large corporate-owned farms are more efficient than small family-owned farms anyway, so the loss would be, well, negligible.

Don't believe the lie some people say that farm subsidies result in food prices which are stable. Let's not forget where all of that money farmers are receiving initially came from . . . That's right. It comes from tax revenues, which were collected from taxpayers such as you and me. Basically, the government is redistributing income for the benefit of farmers. Personally, I'd rather keep the extra money in my pocket and deal with increases in food prices myself. I don't need the government's assistance one bit.

Last, we need to consider the negative effects subsidies have on foreign economies. That's right. I said foreign. You see, selling American crops overseas disrupts foreign economies. Many nations in Africa and Asia have numerous citizens who live on farms and whose livelihoods come from selling crops. When cheap American foodstuffs drive down prices, local farmers lose money, which makes many of them poor and causes others to lose their farms.

Sample Answer

Reading Note

Are advantages to paying subsidies to U.S. farmers

1 provides stability for farmers
    – let them overcome bad harvest or damage from weather and pests
    – can invest in new equipment & try new techniques
    – encourage children to become farmers

2 stabilize food prices
    – prevents glut of food on market
    – keeps farmers from raising prices

3 lets American farmers compete worldwide
    – food prices cheap in other countries
    – subsidies let farmers charge lower prices
    – can be competitive overseas

Listening Note

Subsidies to farmers → should be abolished

1 farmers shouldn't be paid to do no work
    – free market → shouldn't guaranteed people cash for no work
    – don't care about getting children to work on farms
    – corporate-owned farms > family-owned farms

2 subsidy $ comes from taxpayers
    – government redistributing income
    – would rather keep $ and pay higher food prices

3 have negative effect on foreign economies
    – American foodstuffs disrupt foreign economies
    – Africa & Asia → many people live on farms
    – cheap American foodstuffs → drive down prices → farmers lose $ or farms

Sample Essay

The professor's lecture covers what she believes are the numerous drawbacks to subsidies paid to farmers by the American government. In doing so, the professor challenges the claims made in the reading passage that subsidies provide many benefits.

The professor begins by announcing that farmers should not be paid if they fail to do their jobs properly. She states her belief in the free market and says that no subsidies should be given to farmers who do not produce any crops. Her opinion is different from that of the author of the reading passage. The author believes it is important to subsidize farmers in case the weather or pests kill their crops.

Next, the professor points out that the money the government uses to pay farmers comes from taxpayers. She says she would rather have that money in her pocket and pay higher food prices than have that money go to farmers. As a result, she disagrees with the statement in the reading passage that subsidies help keep food prices down.

Lastly, the professor claims that cheap American foodstuffs harm farmers in other countries by driving prices down. She notes that many foreign farmers lose money or their farms because of the low prices. Therefore she disagrees with the claim in the reading passage that subsidies make American farmers competitive overseas.

TASK 2 Independent Writing   p. 146

Sample Answer 1

Agree

fewer drivers on roads
– some can't afford gas + others don't want to pay more $
– fewer cars = less air pollution

tax revenues increase
– can use $ to fight air pollution
– give to people cleaning environment + doing research on pollution
– spend $ on alternative forms of energy

Sample Essay

Air pollution is a huge problem where I live as there is a lot of smog, and it can sometimes be hard to breathe the air. I would love for the government to do something about this situation. I believe that raising the price of gas would be effective at reducing air pollution, so I agree with the statement.

If the government raises the price of gas, then there

will be some people who will drive less. A few of them will not be able to afford to buy gas while others will not want to purchase gas because of the higher price. In both cases, the end result will be fewer cars on the roads. Since not as many people will be driving, there will be fewer cars burning fuel and releasing harmful pollutants into the air. This will almost instantly reduce the amount of air pollution, and, over time, the quality of the air will become much better. As for the people who no longer drive, they can take public transportation such as buses and subways. It might be somewhat inconvenient for them, but their sacrifices will improve the environment.

Another benefit of the government raising the price of gas is that the amount of tax revenues the government receives will increase even though fewer people will be driving. The government should pass a law stating that all revenues raised from this new gas tax will be used to fight air pollution. Some of the money can go to people who are cleaning up the environment. Other funds can go to individuals and groups doing research on how to reduce pollution. And more money can go to those who are working on alternative energy forms such as solar and wind power. Since they do not produce any air pollution at all, the more research done on them, the more efficient those types of energy will become.

The government should definitely increase the price of gasoline to reduce air pollution. Getting more cars off the road will be one advantage, and increased tax revenues will be another. Together, they can improve the quality of the air.

Sample Answer 2

Disagree

won't affect how much people drive
- gas price goes up and down → people still drive
- e.g. high price in the past → parents complained but still drove

government will waste $ raised
- will not use $ to reduce air pollution
- will give $ to companies owned by friends
- government = waste, incompetence, and fraud

Sample Essay

The idea suggested in the statement is horrible, so I completely disagree with it. The government should not raise the price of gas to reduce air pollution. I am against this statement for several reasons, but I shall go into detail on two of them.

To begin with, raising the price of gas will not affect how much people drive since they still need to travel to work and other places. The only result will be that people will have to spend more money on gasoline, so they will have less money to spend on food, housing, and entertainment. We should remember that the price of gas constantly goes up and down. A couple of years ago, it went up an extremely high amount, yet that did not stop my parents from driving as much as they normally do. Nor did it prevent any other people from driving their cars. Everyone, including my parents, simply had to pay the higher rates for gasoline. I remember my parents complaining about that, but they continued driving. That is how I am sure people's driving behavior will not change if the government increases the price of gas.

I am sure there are people who claim that the government will use the increased tax revenues to fight air pollution, but I doubt that will happen. Governments always waste the money they collect from taxes, so I am positive that if the government starts raising billions of dollars more in revenue, politicians will find many ways to spend it improperly. First, they will probably not use the money to reduce air pollution even if they promise the people they will do that. Additionally, they will most likely spend the money on pointless projects that funnel money to companies owned by their friends. I have seen far too many examples of governmental waste, incompetence, and fraud to trust politicians to use the people's money properly.

I disagree with the statement one hundred percent. Raising the price of gasoline will not stop people from driving their cars, and the money that gets raised will be wasted and will not be used to fight air pollution. Raising the price of gasoline is a terrible idea and should not be done.

TASK 1 Integrated Writing

p. 151

Listening Script

Now listen to part of a lecture on the topic you just read about.

M Professor: Let's look at the economics involved in the ongoing conflict in the Congo. One major factor is the wealth the rebels get on account of controlling the eastern part of the country. That area has numerous mines, including coltan mines. Coltan is a raw mineral which can be refined into other materials needed to make various electronics. Many people have called for an end to the purchasing of Congolese coltan, but, well, that's simply not practical right now.

The first reason has to do with the law of supply and demand. Millions of electronic devices are sold around the world each year. Most of them contain some tantalum, which is derived from coltan. Thus the desire for coltan is enormous, and the efforts of some governments to ban the sale of coltan and tantalum are being actively resisted. We should also consider that the big electronics companies don't buy coltan directly from the rebels. Instead, they get it secondhand in the form of tantalum. A large amount of tantalum comes from China. The Chinese frequently mix coltan from different sources and claim that the tantalum they sell isn't made from Congolese coltan. That's a dubious, but, uh, effective claim.

Furthermore, there are other supplies of coltan, but they are not enough to meet the demand for it. Presently, the Congo and nearby Rwanda supply around thirty percent of the world's coltan. Electronics companies require it, so they're not going to stop buying it. And be aware that Australia's and Canada's coltan reserves are dwindling while new coltan mines in Venezuela and Columbia are in regions which are both unstable and in constant conflict. The bottom line is that, well, as long as people want electronics, the rebel-controlled coltan mines in the Congo are going to have customers.

Sample Answer

Reading Note

Coltan mined in Eastern Congo → has bad effect on people there

1 rebel groups control E. Congo

- sell coltan → spend $ on weapons and supplies
- people buying coltan = supporting bloodshed
- governments should ban purchase and importing of Congolese coltan
- should ban sale of tantalum from China → smelts Congolese coltan to make tantalum

2 **don't need to buy coltan from Congo**
- Australia, Canada & Brazil → larger deposits of coltan
- new mines in Venezuela and Columbia
- enough coltan in other countries → should stop buying from Congo

Listening Note

Not practical to ban purchase of Congolese coltan

1 **law of supply and demand**
- huge need for coltan worldwide
- resisting effort to ban Congolese coltan
- don't buy from rebels → buy secondhand as tantalum
- Chinese say isn't from Congo → doubtful but effective

2 **not enough coltan elsewhere**
- Congo + Rwanda = 30% of world's coltan
- Australia & Canada → coltan reserves going down
- Venezuela & Columbia → unstable and in conflicts

Sample Essay

The professor's lecture concerns the mineral coltan, which is mined in the Congo, a country in Africa. While the author of the reading passage argues in favor of the banning of the sale of Congolese coltan, the professor disagrees. He believes it is impractical to ban the sale of coltan from the Congo.

First, the professor cites the law of supply and demand. He declares that the need for it by manufacturers around the world means that Congolese coltan will always have buyers. He notes that companies do not directly buy from the rebels but often get their coltan from China, which, because it mixes coltan from various sources, can claim that it does not sell Congolese coltan. In this way, the professor goes against the argument in the reading passage that the world's governments should ban the sale of coltan from the Congo.

Next, while the author of the reading passage states that there are many other sources of coltan, the professor disputes this notion. He remarks that the coltan reserves of Australia and Canada are decreasing rather than increasing. While he admits that there are new sources of coltan in both Venezuela and Columbia, he points out problems with buying coltan from those places because of their instability. Therefore the professor believes that Congolese coltan is always going to have customers.

TASK 2 Independent Writing p. 156

Sample Answer 1

Agree

do charity work
- many charities can join + volunteer work
- e.g. sis, bro, & me → do volunteer work
- other young people do, too

help others in foreign countries
- e.g. cousin → helps poor children in Africa
- met many young people there

make financial contributions
- have little $ → so small donations
- e.g. typhoon caused damage to villages → many young people donated $ to help

Sample Essay

Nowadays, I see young people constantly devoting their time and effort to helping others. They do this much more than young people in the past ever did. Therefore, I am in agreement with the statement.

There are countless opportunities for young people to engage in charity work these days. There are a large number of charitable organizations that people can join, and there are many opportunities for people to do volunteer work as well. For instance, my sister, brother, and I all do volunteer work at least once a week. I work at a soup kitchen, my sister volunteers at a hospital, and my brother teaches children to read at the local library. We are not unusual as many of the other young people I know similarly volunteer their time to help others.

Young people do not simply help others in their own countries either. Many make an effort to assist people in other countries. My cousin is involved with a charity that aids poor children in Africa. She has worked with people in the organization, and she even traveled to Africa last summer to meet some of the kids she was helping. While she was there, she met lots of other young people from countries around the world. They were doing the same thing she was: spending time helping others.

Modern-day young people also make financial contributions to help others. Most young people do not have part-time jobs, so they can only make small donations to charities and groups trying to help others. Still, they are often eager to make donations. For instance, there was a typhoon in my country recently. It caused a lot of damage to some villages on the coast.

Nearly all of my friends donated as much money as they could to help those people whose lives were affected by the typhoon. They did not have to give money, but they did so out of a desire to help others.

Young people have many chances to assist others these days, they can help people in foreign countries, and they are often obligated to do so by their schools. When those three factors are combined, the result is that young people clearly devote more time and effort to helping others than youths did in the past.

Sample Answer 2

Disagree

parents did volunteer work
- volunteered as teens
- worked at hospital → met there while volunteering
- many other teens volunteered, too

young people traveled abroad as missionaries
- grandfather → went to South America
- were young missionaries from many other places

helped neighbors a lot
- grandparents & parents → helped neighbors in various ways
- people today → rarely help neighbors

Sample Essay

It is true that young people today regularly engage in work that can improve the world. However, I know that young people in the past also devoted a large amount of their time to doing the same thing, so I disagree with the statement.

My parents are a perfect example of how youths in the past dedicated time and effort to improving the world. Both of my parents were heavily involved in volunteer work when they were teenagers. While they did not have the opportunity to travel abroad, they spent a great amount of time working in their own country. In fact, that was how they met. They were doing volunteer work at a local hospital when they met as teens. They have told me that there were numerous other people their age who volunteered at various places as well.

In the past, large numbers of young people traveled abroad to serve as missionaries. My grandfather was a Christian missionary in South America when he was in his early twenties. He did that several decades ago. He was not the only young person who was a missionary as well. Not only did young people from my country work as missionaries, but people from many other countries also traveled abroad to do the same thing. When my grandfather received training to become a missionary, he was accompanied by young people from countries all around the world.

Finally, people in the past used to help others, particularly their neighbors, much more than people do today. My grandparents have told me stories about how they assisted their neighbors in various ways when they were young. My parents acted in a similar manner as well. Any time their neighbors had problems, many people—both young and old alike—visited them and did their best to provide assistance to solve their problems. People—especially young ones—almost never do that today.

Young people in the past often spent time and effort to try to improve the world. They did at least as much as young people today do. For those reasons, I must disagree with the statement.

Memo